THE LIGHT OF DARKNESS

The Light of Darkness

The Story of the Griots' Son

Alhassan Susso

Edited by Kevin Morris

2016

Copyright © 2016 by Alhassan Susso

Published by Alhassan Susso

The Susso Academy

Poughkeepsie, New York 12601

Website: www.alhassansusso.com

Email: alhassansusso@gmail.com

Printed in the United States of America

First printing: July 2016

Cover design: Mory Rivera

Interior design: Bintou Susso

Summary: A practical and inspirational story of striving for higher consciousness and an in-depth look at the meaning of obstacles and steps to overcome them.

ISBN-13: 978-0692754658

Praise for *The Light of Darkness*

When I met Alhassan 16 years ago, he was a young boy just arriving in America with a rare eye disease. Despite facing such a harsh medical prognosis, he exhibited unusual grace and charm for someone his age. Now that I have read his memoir, *The Light of Darkness*, I have come to better understand his wisdom and depth. I enjoyed learning about his country, his culture, and the values he was raised on. You will certainly enjoy this moving story. You can see how, even with limited eyesight, Alhassan has great vision and insight into the human character and the human condition. I strongly recommend this beautiful book.

- Dr. James Cayea

Optometrist, Dutchess Optometry

I am proud of how well my son has picked up the mantle he has inherited from me and my forefathers, the griot tradition of storytelling. I am proud of his growth, tenacity and desire to transform the lives of others as his life has been transformed. The Light of Darkness tells our family story, but much more than that, it tells the story of our people and all people in the human family. From the dirt roads of The Gambia to the bright lights of New York City, Alhassan paints the most vibrant pictures of both worlds and he shares his views on the meaning of life and the purpose of helping others along the way.

- Alhaji Papa Susso

The Griot

Dedication

This book is dedicated to my daughter, Amina Susso and her namesake, Namie, my Grandmother.

Amina, thank you for your patience for the countless hours I was not home to be with you. Since we welcomed you home three years ago, our house became complete. Your charming and uplifting attitude gives your mother and me something to look forward to every day. I can't wait to see the great woman you'll grow up to be. I do know one thing for sure: you'll do great things in this world.

Namie, every day feels like you're still with me. While you're in a better place, I miss you a lot. The humility, gratitude, and sense of purpose you instilled in me are still the core tenets of my life. For everything you have done for me,

THANK YOU!

Foreword

In early autumn of 2000, I was introduced to a young man with an electric smile and sparkling eyes. He had just arrived from The Gambia, West Africa, and was brought to meet me by his older brother, who had been a friend of mine for several years. This young man, Alhassan "Las" Susso, was 16 years old at the time, and was embarking on a new life in America.

I was more than happy to be of assistance to him when I could -- advice with homework, long drives to introduce him to the beauty and the history of the Hudson Valley, talks about plans and choices in life, and many pleasant meals at home and around town. As I came to know him, his intellect, seriousness and generous spirit, his industriousness and reliability became more and more evident to me. But I also began to learn more and more from him.

Of course, he helped me understand something of the cultures and politics of West Africa. But more importantly, over the 16 years I have known him, I have come to know more about the trials in his own personal history, the deep responsibility to an African family on two continents, and the hidden constraints he had to cope with daily.

The short story of how Las has moved through life may seem on the surface easy -- success in a tough city high school, the first taste of higher education at the local community college, going on to a four-year college in Vermont where his wife had an impressive job, and then to graduate school, followed by a teaching job. But that superficially easy-sounding biography hides many challenges and hurdles.

This book describes these things, which he modestly calls "frustrations." It turns out that Las is a very fine story teller, and I found myself drawn into not only episodes that I already knew about, but also many events that he had not told me about before. But a list of the difficulties isn't the point of this book, though it is important to understand the rough interactions, the continual limitations, and the demands of extended family life.

More importantly the book describes how Las drew insights from his frustrations, constraints, and losses, and how he thoughtfully and consistently worked to turn those insights into opportunities. This capacity has proven to be one of the most impressive things I now know about Las. His episodes of struggle and adaptation have not been easy, but his development over time of an effective philosophy and practice from extracting opportunity from frustration is an inspiration to me. I suspect that many people will draw strength and strategy from his story.

Although Las's stories are personal and his own, they resonate broadly. Among the themes that appear are some that are universal or very widely felt: the immigrant experience, the discovery of what it means to be Black in America, the numbness of repetitive jobs, the uncertainty of deciding on a career path in college, the difference between being educated to be a teacher and actually being one, the power of faith, and the burden of prejudice of many kinds.

I am happy to say that I feel some responsibility for this book. Our many conversations about life, work, and leisure (less of that than the others!) led me to suggest that Las should write up his experiences, insights, and novel educational strategies that emerged from teaching government and history in an international high school in the Bronx. But how to explain that without first explaining Las's own experiences as an immigrant, as initially an outsider in America, as one who had both internal and external obstacles to overcome?

That need is the source of the book you now hold -- that and Las's generosity in wanting to share with people some of the ideas and practices that have helped him overcome those obstacles. Although there are many stories and events here that are touched with pathos, the thing that comes through most strongly to me is the joy of turning obstacles into opportunities, and then the joy in sharing the lessons learned. Every time Las and I talk about these joys, I see the flash of that electric smile, and the sparkle in his eye. Enjoy this wonderful little book.

Dr. Steward T.A. Pickett,

Poughkeepsie

Preface

In the spring of 2015, I noticed a change in one of my students. She looked a bit more somber than usual. For a moment, I thought she was simply having a difficult time preparing the final projects for graduation. But as I watched this child with her head constantly down, I could not help but wonder if something beyond the pressures of completing her graduation requirements was going on. I called her in for a conversation and all of a sudden, she broke down in tears. As it turned out, she was kicked out of the house by her mother and she was also battling a health challenge. As we explored options, we talked about looking at the issue from a different angle. She could use her circumstance as an excuse or as a reason to succeed.

We all experience an ongoing struggle or a severe pain at some point in our lives. The only question is: what kind of person would we become at the end of the story? Would we become bitter or would we become better? While my student's condition was extremely difficult, with the proper support, she was able to overcome that challenge by making choices that empowered her. Therefore, it was fulfilling when this student crossed the stage last year and received her diploma. "I've come out better, Mr. Alhassan." Seeing the transformation and the eventual graduation of this particular student sparked the idea of this book.

As a high school history teacher in the South Bronx, I get to work with kids with social, emotional, as well as family challenges on a daily basis. At the age of 16, I migrated to the U.S. and I have lived through some of the same experiences. Therefore, I was able to help a significant number of my students overcome their varying struggles by sharing my stories, experiences and lessons. Because this helped so many of my students to chart a better path for their lives, I believe that many others beyond the walls of my classroom could benefit as well.

It was through these experiences, failures and successes of my students that I realized that there is nothing broken about anyone. Our biggest challenge, however, is having the necessary skills or having to learn from others' stories who have been through a similar situation. My conversations with my students during their times of trials are to strive for something bigger than themselves. Our lives are either going to be an example or a warning.

When I initially embarked on the journey to write this book, my focus was on my life's obstacles and my daily struggles with a health challenge. But as I reflect deeper on my life and everything that contributed to propelling me to where I am today, I realized that there is more to my life than a health challenge. The people I grew up with, the places I've visited and lived in, the experiences I've come to see, and the lessons I've learned, all contributed to making me who I am today. Therefore, while the objective of this book is to explore my secret health frustrations and how I turned those frustrations into opportunities for a higher calling, this book will explore further than that single story of struggle.

Part I will introduce you to my griot roots in The Gambia, to my Gambian family, culture, and education system.

Part II looks at my transition from The Gambia into an American high school student and the trials and triumphs that come with being a recent immigrant maneuvering a deep and cosmopolitan society.

Part III examines the obstacles and blessing that come with living in a complex and dynamic society with regards to race, culture, the education system and my personal challenges of being an immigrant with a disability.

Part IV traces my journey into becoming a teacher and a father. More importantly, this section looks at how my yet brief life comes into a full circle at this stage despite the detours and mountains I had to climb.

Finally, Part V evaluates and reflects on the key people, moments and experiences that have guided me over the last 30 years.

To protect the privacy of certain individuals and places, pseudonyms were typically used for episodes that were unpleasant. But I am also honored to recognize and celebrate the remarkable people, places and experiences that fully led to where I am in life today.

Let's begin!

If we stand tall, it is because we stand on the backs of those who came before us. --Yoruba Proverb

Introduction

As I sit down to record these brief memories from my yet brief life, I can't help but reflect on my father, his father and a long line of griots, who came before me, passing history down son to son, like a runner in a relay race passing the baton; the urgency and obligation delicately placed into the hands of the one who must run the next leg, the next generation, toward a finish line still too distant to be seen around the sharp bend of history.

The griot, like the relay runner, is the caretaker of something both precious and fragile, and without which the race cannot be won unless it is delivered whole and complete to the next generation, and the race begins anew, as long as history continues to unfold and be told.

In the simplest of terms, a *griot* is a West African storyteller, but as this story will show, the griot plays a much more complex role than retelling stories of the old. It is that meaning, and the purpose handed down to me from father to son – and sometimes mother to son – that this book is in part about, and while I don't yet hold the title of griot, I am one by birth and by inheritance, and the human urge implanted in me has molded every aspect of my life so far: my choices, my surroundings, my travels, my fears, my hopes, my lessons, my values, my profession and my faith and beliefs, some part of which I plan to share with you in this story.

This story is about family and lineage. It is about tradition and change. It is about Africa, in a sense, if there is really such a place as singular in definition as Africa. It certainly is a story about being African, particularly from the perspective of my new American family.

This story is also about seeing and awareness, and conversely about blindness and ignorance. It's about what we can see, what we are conditioned to see, and what we can learn to see. It is about blind spots and the search for higher consciousness: culturally, historically, personally, professionally, economically, religiously, and otherwise. For sight, both symbolically and biologically, is a central theme of my story, as you will come to see, pun intended.

And yes, it is a story about the importance of storytelling, of remembrance, of the obligation to remember and to retell, and of course the warning not to forget. It is about the power of story to bind a people together so tightly even the harshest of circumstances (war, poverty, disease, dislocation) cannot destroy their sense of identity and unity as a people. In that sense – story serves as a cultural survival tool. This story is for everyone, anyone striving for a deeper understanding of the meaning of life and the challenges of translating that meaning into a life both personally fulfilling and meaningful to the great human society.

What I had taken for granted before I embarked on this journey has become so much clearer to see. I am delighted to share some of the short stories of my life and my reflections on what those stories meant to me and more importantly, the potential of how my experience can shed light on the lives of others, facing similar and separate circumstances. For no matter how far I travel nor old I get, I am and will always be the griots' son. Here are some glimpses into my life, as such.

Map of Africa

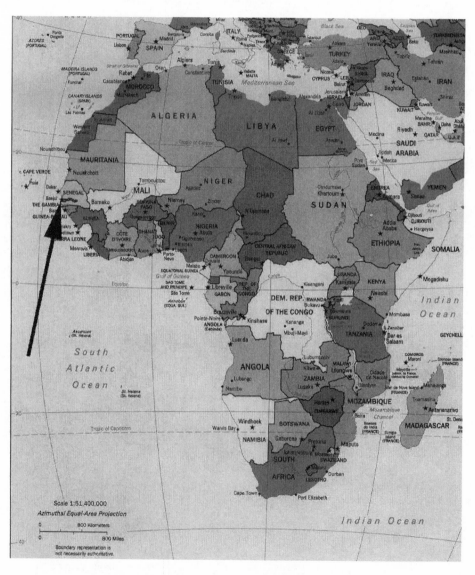

http://www.lahistoriaconmapas.com/atlas2/africa+map/gambia-africa-map.htm

Map of The Gambia

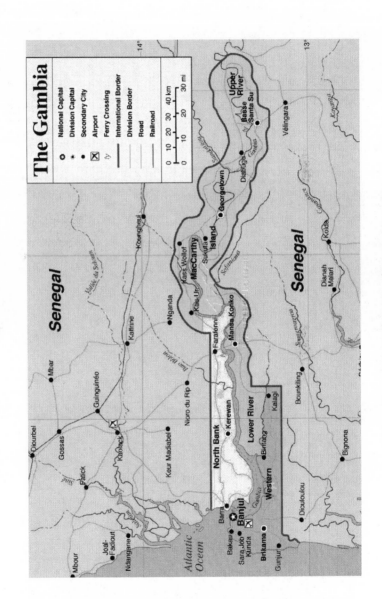

PART I

If there is no enemy within, the enemy outside can do us no harm

--African Proverb

Blinded by the Light

As the sun was setting on a bright and clear day, I was running with my friends to come back home from the playground as we did every evening. As usual, we were singing, dancing and having the time of our lives as every kid does at that age.

The only difference however, was this was not just any day or any kid. Little did I know that I would remember this day for the rest of my life. It was a day I would like to forget, but it is a part of what made me who I am today.

"You dropped your "Talla" (a Gambian coin). I looked down and the coin was nowhere to be seen.

"Where is it?" I asked.

"Right there," my friends replied, pointing to the ground.

I looked all over my surroundings, but the money was, again, nowhere to be found. After this went on for several seconds, the children began to snicker and giggle. It was not funny to me at all. The only adult among us was Amie, who was staying with my family for the summer. She also started laughing. As the laughs continued, the coin was still on the ground.

Everyone present could see it except me. All of a sudden, I began to realize that something might be different with my vision. It was at this point that the dilemma of whether something was wrong with my vision became crystal clear when Amie finally picked up the coin, which was right by my left foot, and said,

"Las is blind" (Las is my nickname).

When she mentioned this, all the kids burst into a huge laughter. As I put the money in my pocket, standing there embarrassed and humiliated, I did not know what to do or how to feel. I simply walked into the compound and went straight to the bathroom to take a shower.

I was raised by my Grandmother, Namie. A woman who gave me hope when there seemed to be none. A woman who instilled in me everything that made me who I am today. She was a woman who would never call anybody by their name, but would always have a sweet slogan to make the person's name sound like a song. Whenever she would call your name, no matter what mood you happened to be in, she would increase your spirit and energy. She would always go out of her way to ensure she was a blessing to others through her words and actions.

I learned from her that one thing all human beings need is to feel appreciated. Namie ensured that she would cheer up anyone who came across her path. I will be sharing a lot of lessons I learned from my grandmother throughout the book. Her words of wisdom transformed relationships for the better; her electrifying energy lifted spirits; her charisma was certainly inspiring to an entire generation; but more importantly, her treatment of every single person regardless of age, gender or social status with respect and dignity has allowed me, and countless other people, to understand our bond of humanity.

Elegant and charismatic, she stood at 5 feet, 9 inches tall. Her glamour attracted anyone in close proximity. Namie was born and raised in Sotuma. She grew up in the family of griots and carried the tradition.

Yes, my grandmother, like my father, my mother and most of my forefathers, was a griot, a fact which meant very little to me as a child. I didn't know it then, but her sharp voice, compassion, and electrifying smile made her one of the most revered griots in The Gambia.

All I knew about this great griot was that she was my beloved grandmother. While she served her community from time to time, particularly during important cultural events (weddings, naming ceremonies, circumcisions, feasts, anniversaries, etc.), her main occupation was family rearing. In addition to her own children, she raised all of her grandchildren, numbering eight boys and three girls.

She had two children, my mother and her sister Jukuna. But Jukuna passed away in the late 1970s so, by the time I was born, my mom was her only remaining daughter.

According to Namie, Jukuna passed away due in part to physical and mental abuse by her husband, so Namie did everything possible to alleviate as much stress as possible for my mother. Raising kids is obviously both a blessing and a challenge. Namie took care of us so my mother could focus on her "wifely" duties around the house as well as keeping up with her griot tradition.

Namie's husband was Malang Jobarteh, a well-respected griot in his time. He had passed away prior to my birth, so the only things I know of him are the stories I learned from my mother and grandmother. He was a strict controller who did not give his wives opportunities to live a normal life. His jealousy and iron-fist style of running his house was deeply despised by my grandmother. After his death, Namie did not re-marry for a long time. She certainly did not want to repeat the struggles of her first marriage.

Namie's second husband was Saikou Jobarteh. Saikou was perhaps one of the friendliest, kind-hearted, loving and admired individuals that I've ever known. His gentleness and respect for all human beings clearly brought out the best in my grandmother. Growing up, I always admired their affection for each other and their relationship was an early example for me about the meaning of a loving and harmonious relationship. Every journey, however, must come to an end; Saikou passed away in 1998. His passing left a scar in my grandmother's heart from which I don't think she ever recovered.

My grandmother's father was Bamba Susso. The most respected griot of his generation. The African Studies departments of many universities in the U.S. have a record of his stories and narration of history. He was one of few griots to have a national weekly broadcast radio show in The Gambia.

My grandmother was the foundation and cement of our family: keeping us safe, together and thriving. Despite my grandmother's superb emotional intelligence, there was nothing she or anybody could say to me on the night I learned I was "blind," to calm me down. I was sad and confused. But, more than anything, I was determined to understand whether my eyes were different. In other words, was I really "blind?"

As soon as Namie came from the mosque for the sunset prayer, I approached her walking despondently towards her, with my head down and tears in my eyes. "What's wrong?" she asked, because it was obvious that something was terribly wrong.

"Am I blind?"

I wasn't going to sugarcoat anything. All I needed was a confirmation.

As a four year old child, I did not know, nor could I fully grasp the meaning of blindness. But I did know this much that night: something was drastically different about my vision from that of my peers.

Grandma's first response was, "Who told you that?"

I replied, "Amie." That was the first and probably the only time that I've seen my grandmother furious. While it looked like she had some interesting choice words, she quickly held back. I would later understand my grandmother's reservation from confronting Amie. In our Mandinka culture, guests must be treated with the utmost of respect and reverence.

All she said then was, "Amie, that was not nice." She then held my hand and we walked into the living room.

"What makes you special in this world, 'Brusselinko'" (that's how she called me: meaning the guy who would own diamonds in the future), "is not your vision or your other physical characteristics, but rather your kindness to others. And that's what you should focus on."

"Well, Namie, is Amie right? Am I blind?"

She paused for a second, thinking about how to come up with language that would not be demoralizing, but at the same time, would be truthful. She was now caught in a delicate balance between moral values and being a good parent.

"No, you're not blind." I thought for a second I was fine.

Then these words followed after a pause: "You just happen to see differently, which is absolutely fine."

At this point I was again, more confused.

"Different? How?" I said to my grandmother.

"Well, every one of us is unique in our own way."

The phrases I heard that night and beyond was, "We're all born with all the necessary tools to accomplish a race that has been designed for us." As a child, I had no clue what this meant, but I would realize later in life the importance of this statement.

That night, nearly thirty years ago, marked the beginning of a new reality for me. This was the beginning of a journey unknown. Unknown, because I had so many more questions than answers. But one thing was certain; I was entering a new chapter. A chapter that I was not sure how it would end.

This new chapter brought fear, isolation, uncertainty, and sadly, a sense of inferiority. This badge of inferiority has shaped my identity, especially during my childhood.

On that fateful night at the age of four, I gave myself a new identity based on a belief that I was made "less than," or God made a mistake with me. These thoughts would become my reality.

Homebound

As I gave myself this new identity, I refrained from all social gatherings. Every day, all of us make choices, whether consciously or subconsciously. The first conscious choice I made from that moment on was to not go outside after sunset because I couldn't see at night. While I had not gone to a doctor to examine my eyes, I managed to get by during the day, except during bright sunny days. The night darkness frightened me for several reasons: I was frightened by risk of injuring myself, of course, but more so by having my blindness, my inescapable weakness, made known to others. I wanted to keep people blind about my blindness.

But nighttime isolation posed a particular social problem for me. I grew up in a community that is very socially engaged. Nighttime is typically when friends would gather and talk, play, simply have fun. My childhood was spent in hiding. As my friends would meet to discuss the events of the day, I was sitting on my grandmother's lap, listening to her sing and tell me folktales and stories. Songs that had no meaning to me and no relevance in my life at the time, or folktales that my friends found "weird." Little did I know that those "weird" songs, folktales, stories and examples were preparing me for my future destiny. You see, my grandmother was being my griot, telling me the stories and lessons of life.

However, the consequences of staying at home after sunset were preventing me from getting my wishes at the time. It was more than staying home at night. The conscious choice that I made about staying home at night robbed me of the pleasures I deserved to enjoy at that age.

For example, hanging out with my friends would have developed my interpersonal skills as well as allow me to enjoy the pleasures that come with being a kid. I was irritated when my friends laughed or made fun of me for being a Grandma's boy. I would have loved to hang out with my friends at night just as we did during the day, but I was scared of what might happen. It always saddened me when they were making their nighttime plans, and all of sudden one of them would say, "Well, let's not count on Grandma's boy."

One day, I unfortunately happened to stay at my parents' house to eat before going to bed at my grandmother's. On my way to my grandmother's, I heard a bicycle bell sound behind me in the dark. I moved to the left side of the street to avoid collision, but the bell kept ringing. I quickly moved to the right side, but the bell sound became louder and closer and then, all of a sudden, I was on the ground. I heard this loud voice "What is wrong with you? Don't you look to see where you are going?" Hoping not to get beaten up by this individual who I could not see, I quickly got up from the ground and cleaned the sand off of me and apologized to him. Luckily I was not physically hurt from the bicycle collision, but it left a mental scar about the meaning of going out at night.

On another occasion, I was walking from my parent's house to my grandmother's during a very bright sunny day, and without seeing where I was going, I walked straight into the corrugated fence of one of our neighbors and the right side of my forehead was slit open. After spending four hours at the emergency room, I came out with twelve stitches. These two experiences had a profound impact on my reluctance to leave the house at night.

Griot Roots

I was born in The Gambia in West Africa. The Gambia is a country mostly surrounded by Senegal with a short strip of its coastline bordered with the Atlantic Ocean at its western end. It is the smallest country on mainland Africa.

The Gambia is situated on either side of the River Gambia, the nation's namesake, which flows through the center of The Gambia and empties into the Atlantic Ocean. Its area is about 4000 square miles with a population of about two million. Banjul is The Gambian capital, and the largest cities are Serekunda and Brikama.

The Gambia shares historical roots with many other West African nations in the slave trade, which was the key factor in the placing and keeping of a colony on The Gambia River, first by the Portuguese. In 1765, The Gambia was made a part of the British colony when the government formally assumed control, establishing the Province of Senegambia. On 18 February 1965, The Gambia gained independence from the United Kingdom.

There are eight main ethnic groups in The Gambia living side by side with a minimal inter-tribal friction, each preserving its own language, music, cultural traditions and even caste systems, though, there is an increasing amount of cultural interaction.

Each of these communities speaks their own language -- all of which are classified as part of the Niger-Congo language group. The single largest ethnic group in The Gambia is the Mandinka or Mandingos, an agricultural people with hereditary nobility.

My family descended from the Mandinkas, going back more generations than I can count. My father is a griot, the last in a line perhaps, but that story is still unfolding. He was aptly named, *Papa*, in honor of his grandfather, also a griot. His father was Bunka Susso and his mother was Mariama Susso, also griots.

My grandparents and parents' birth village is Sotuma, located in the vast rural area of The Gambia, about 150 miles from the capital. It is a small village with about 300 residents at the time. The people were farmers and grew their own food. The houses were small huts with no indoor plumbing. There was no electricity or tap water. The five major compounds comprising five family groups were: Touray kunda (Islamic Scholars), Sankanula (Governors), Jali kunda (the Griots), Nomoluya (the Blacksmiths) and Tumarankeh (the New-Comers). Our family was a part of the Jali kunda group.

Unique to Western Africa, the griot plays many roles -- more than just a storyteller, he or she is a genealogist, singer, deliverer of social or diplomatic messages and war rouser. Griots often play a central role in various tribal celebrations. Taught by their elders over many years, griots learn the canon of traditional songs, melodies and rhythms. Traditionally, in order to become a griot, you had to be born into a griot family, as I was.

The griot tradition has proved remarkably resilient in West Africa, seven centuries after its beginnings during the Malinke Empire which stretched from modern day Senegal to Timbuktu and Gao in Mali and even included parts of Côte d'Ivoire. Even though they are highly respected and paid well for their services, griots belong in one of the lower castes of society.

Griots often traveled far and wide to sing praises to wealthy and powerful patrons, as did my father, who served a prominent businessman in Liberia named Sankung Bayo for several years. When his patron died, my father returned to The Gambia in 1982. While in The Gambia, he worked for the government as an accountant for years. In 1986, Papa left The Gambia for the United States.

Old Jeshwang was the town where both my grandmother and my parents ended up settling after leaving Sotuma. Old Jeshwang is a small town of about 20 thousand people. While it was a town, there were no street lights, and the only road that was paved was the main highway. This made getting around after sunset virtually impossible for me.

My mother's name is Sarjo Jobarteh. She grew up in a griot family in Sotuma. She bore seven children (Bunka, Sankung, Fatou, Alhassan, Mamie, Binta, and Kinda). Two of the children (Bunka and Mamie) passed away before the age of 1, and Binta passed away at 19 years old.

My mother was not my father's only wife, as polygamy is acceptable in our culture. My father had a total of five wives. Though he had only two wives at any given time, it is not uncommon for Gambian men to have several wives at once. The first wife, by tradition, is the most important wife and maintains the highest standing of all subsequent wives.

Mom, (Na, as we call mothers in The Gambia) made a living through her griot tradition by singing praises to people at ceremonial events such as weddings, naming ceremonies, etc. Despite facing tremendous challenges, she always persevered regardless of the obstacles. Her mantra is: "If you keep doing the right thing, God will fight your battles." And, "Whatever people expect from you; do twice more." Her patience and forgiving heart has been a source of guidance for me.

My father, Alhaji Papa Susso on the Kora

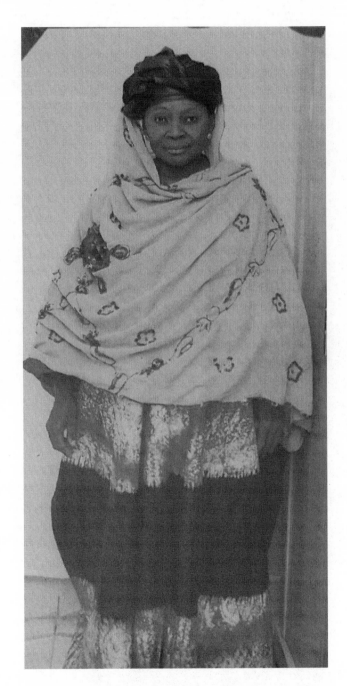

My mother, Sarjo Jobarteh

School

Attending school brought its own challenges with regard to fully engaging with my fellow students. Should I let my teachers know of my condition? Should I be engaged in extracurricular activities? What would happen if people at school find out that I could not clearly see the board and could not see at all at night? These were the questions swirling in the back of my mind while getting ready for school.

I attended school in a cement brick building with corrugated steel roofing. It had 18 classrooms, and about 35 students per class. The chalkboard was black. We had no electricity. It was a strictly lecture based instruction with constant attention to the teacher. The school began promptly at 8:30am and dismissed at 2pm. The school was quarter of a mile from my grandmother's house, so I didn't have to walk that much compared to some of my classmates who would walk three miles or more to come to school.

I did not feel the pain of my vision impairment the first two years of schooling.

However, during third grade, I happened to have a crush on a very pretty, smart and outgoing girl, but had the biggest fear to pursue her. In The Gambia, students' progress is measured by standardized test scores. The way students get promoted from one grade to the next is also through passing of those excruciating exams -- excruciating, because those exams have prevented certain students from achieving their full God-given potential.

For example, one of my best friends, Lamin, was not a good test taker. In The Gambia, if you lack this skill, you are bound for failure in school. Weak test-takers were labeled "stupid," "not intelligent" or "inferior." Regardless of how capable you are in other areas of intelligence, such as problem solving skills, analytical skills, argumentative skills, or, for that matter, interpersonal skills; all that mattered, unfortunately, was the score you received on those exams.

Despite Lamin's great argumentative, analytical and interpersonal skills, he was not even able to complete elementary school because he was unable to pass those exams.

Unfortunately, Lamin was not the only victim of this unjust educational structure; his sister also fell victim to the same system. His sister's highest level of education was the fourth grade because she could not pass the exams. It breaks my heart whenever I visit The Gambia and see Lamin's family's dire situation, due, in part, to the indignities of a system that categorized people based on one element rather than as a whole.

Even with my vision challenges, I was fortunate that I happened to be a strong test taker. So I was considered among the "smart" students. This skill shielded me from being looked down on. Instead, I was treated as special, because I was "intelligent." I always came in first or second place in ranking on every exam during my elementary school years.

In fact, I only came in second place once behind Tuti, the pretty girl I had a crush on. We'd become competitors and secret admirers of each other. But our relationship never took off because I had this fear that if she would ever find out about my condition, she would definitely break up with me. This constant worry prevented me from developing friendships or intimate relationships. While my fellow students, including Tuti, looked up to me and admired me, I was looking down on myself because I thought I was made less than.

The biggest annual festivity during elementary school was the celebration of Commonwealth Day. This is a celebration by formerly British controlled nations as recognition of their membership in the Commonwealth. On this day, all the students would make special dishes and wear the most beautiful attire they owned. This was the day that boys would also express their feelings to the girls they had a crush on. The after party usually happened at night. While all my friends were out partying, I was hiding in the house.

My middle-school experience was similar to that of elementary school. Middle school years are those critical formative years when teenagers are discovering their identity. As I began to think critically about my identity, I'd fully convinced myself that my vision problem defined who I was and how I should behave instead of being defined by everything that fully formed me.

The class you were assigned in my middle school depended upon your score from the "Common Entrance Examination." Common Entrance Examination is the English West African standardized test for sixth graders. Your score on this exam determined the middle school in which you would be placed. Due to my outstanding academic achievement, I was placed in Class A, which is comprised of the highest performing students in the school.

During middle-school, I thrived academically. Nonetheless, the thoughts of not measuring up to others continued to haunt me. As I sat down in the classroom, I was constantly afraid that the teacher might call on me to read the instructions on the board, which was a usual practice at that school. If this was to happen, I would be very embarrassed because I would not be able to read from the board. Even though I sat in front of the class, I still had trouble clearly reading from the board. Our classroom had no electric light inside because people thought there was enough sunlight to see the board. The sunlight was good enough for those who had good eyesight, but I needed more than just sunlight coming into the room. What I needed was a bright light in addition to the sunlight.

The other source of worry during my schooling days in The Gambia was notebook checks. This was also a normal practice at my school, but it was something I was protected from. My class notes were not the most accurate since I only took notes based on what the teacher explained and not what's written on the board. Looking back now, I realize, I've always been guided and shielded by a power higher than mine.

Future Wife

Have you ever been in a situation in which you encountered someone you felt was the right person for you? Or, something occurred and you realized within you it was the right thing to do, have or be. Sometimes we called these moments a "coincidence." The truth of the matter is that we use the word coincidence as a linguistic representation of something we could not naturally conceive.

While our human abilities have limitations in understanding things beyond our imagination, that does not mean that there aren't other abilities beyond our comprehension. Therefore, this concept of coincidence is misrepresented. Coincidence is simply a strategic plan put forward by a higher power to begin the process of propelling you to your next level or to your planned destiny.

This strategic plan called coincidence occurred in my life the summer of 1998 at the end of the 6th Grade. On a Friday afternoon around 3pm, I was throwing a soccer ball on the wall while talking with my mother, who was lying down on a mat on the floor. All of a sudden, this beautiful girl with a pony tail walked into our compound and asked for my little half-sister, Mariama. I was stunned as to her beauty and eloquence. She did not stay for long because my sister was not home at the time. Right after she left, I told my mother without hesitation, "That girl will be my wife." My Mom asked, "What was her name again?" I said her name was "Bintou."

Can you imagine the first thing I did when my sister got home? "Who is Bintou?" I asked. "Why?" She replied. My little sister was someone who gives me lots of grief about everything. "Bintou came looking for you this afternoon. How well do you know her?" I asked. She replied, "Why do you care?" I replied, "Well, she is very beautiful. Could you hook us up?"

It appeared as if someone just tickled Mariama. She started laughing uncontrollably as if I just uttered the world's funniest joke. After about a minute or so of laughter, she finally said, "Boy, you don't stand a chance. So don't even bother."

That fall, Bintou transferred to Methodist Academy, a school located not far from my house. On my way back from school, I always purposefully came home on the same route so I could bump into her on the street. We would simply stare at each other without saying a word. This pattern continued until I left The Gambia for the United States.

Disabled or Abled?

While I was ashamed of my vision problem, the reality was that the culture I grew up in equates disability with inferiority, as if it was your own fault or you must have done something to deserve it. For instance, when I was 11 years old, I went to the hospital in secret, hoping that they would be able to help me with this problem. As I sat in the row for hours waiting to be seen, I was trembling because it would be the first time I would ever explain to anyone what my real condition was.

When it was my turn to see the doctor, I was called in and asked: "What brought you here today?" I was silent for a second, not knowing how this doctor would react. I finally told him I have a vision problem. "What do you mean you've a vision problem?" "I cannot see at night." "What do you mean?" In a loud sturdy voice, the doctor kept on going, "A small boy like you, you cannot see?" "How did you get here if you could not see?" "Where are your parents?" As this doctor continued to bombard me with questions, I regretted going to the hospital. I knew the doctors might not take me seriously because I was young and my condition was unusual. After questioning me for a few minutes and looking confused, the doctor took a flashlight and started examining my eyes.

After just couple of minutes, he wrote me a prescription and said, I could not find anything wrong with your vision, but this might help you. While I did not fully comprehend my visual condition, I did however understand that that prescription was not the answer. I left that hospital more discouraged than ever. If the doctors could not fully comprehend or sympathize with my situation, imagine the rest of society who were naturally insensitive to conditions that are considered abnormal.

If doctors didn't understand, how could my teachers? Knowing the environment and culture, I knew that if I told my teachers my condition, instead of finding ways to help me, I would have probably been categorized under "abnormal people." Rather, I decided to live my life as normal as possible even though I constantly lived in fear, sorrow and believed that my humiliation day at school could be any moment. Therefore, rather than asking for help for the writings on the board, I listened for the explanations from the teachers. This method of learning ended up helping me as I maneuvered through middle school. I managed to successfully complete seventh and eighth grade without embarrassment. Instead, I was again viewed as a "smart student" who strived to attain outstanding academic achievement. I continued to do what I became a master of: keeping people around me blind about my blindness.

While my academic achievements were great, my social relations were not that enticing. Rather than having meaningful and intimate friendships with other students, I stayed as far away as possible because I knew I did not have what it takes to maintain a friendship. Part of what friends did was hanging out in the evening and on weekends visiting and spending nights at each other's houses. To avoid having to explain why I could not do any of those, I simply decided to do what I thought was best: Be by myself.

During middle-school in The Gambia, sporting events were the most exciting times of the year. Athletes also happened to be the most popular students in school. Unfortunately for me, sporting games tend to run into the evening. Therefore, I never attended any of my school games.

The biggest celebration every year in middle school is the championship games, called "inter-house," which takes place at the national stadium. This is the day of celebration and reflection on the year. It is also a day when students show support and pride for their school. But more importantly, it represents the building of lifelong relationships, and provides a showing of solidarity. It typically starts with going to school in the morning for a half day. When school is dismissed, people then get ready to go to the stadium in the afternoon and evening. When the games are over, students tend to head to the beach for the nighttime party. The day began and ended for me at school.

Regardless of how much my friends would encourage me to attend, I always gave them excuses. Never a real excuse, but something that would get me off the hook. They ended up labeling me "anti-social." While this title did not bother me at the beginning, it would later become part of my identity; an identity that I was neither proud of nor wished for; an identity that would neither prosper me nor bring out the best of me. But, this identity kept me safe from being potentially humiliated.

Coming of Age

There were 32 people staying at my grandmother's house. It was an eight-room compound that housed multiple families. One of the residents was a tenant, but this tenant did not pay rent for the 16 years that I lived there. Not only did my grandmother not evict them but also provided them food whenever they could not afford it. While my grandmother's financial resources were modest, her compound was filled with joy, laughter and love. At least four different families were living in this small place, but, if you were a visitor, you would not know the difference.

My grandmother worked so hard to ensure everyone was taken care of, but more importantly, that there was a smile on everyone's faces. However, one day, as we were sitting in the compound, a couple of teenage girls were passing by and we happened to hear one tell the other, "This compound is what makes this street look less appealing."

This was in part because, while grandmother did her best to build that compound with limited resources, the compound was not comparable to the others. For example, the fence was made of corrugated steel, which only low income compounds had, and there were just too many people living in that small place. While it was physically small for the number of people who lived there, what you could not see from behind the fence was all the love, joy and happiness that came from within that small place. The head of that household's belief was: live life to the fullest in every moment regardless of your situation.

While I was a young boy during this time, I had a burning desire to do better in life financially. The girls' comments gave me the understanding that life is mostly based on perception. While we were living happily and enjoying our lives, others felt sorry for us. The desire to rebuild my grandmother's house to be comparable to that of the neighbors would become a mission for me.

My beloved grandmother, Namie

PART II

When the door closes, you must learn to slide across the crack of the sill
--Yoruba Proverb

The Septic Tank

One of the biggest challenges for me living in The Gambia was the rainy season. The rainy season starts in June and lasts till the end of September. Because there was no sewage system to drain the water, all the rain water was stagnant on the street. This was a difficult time for me to maneuver around because I would walk in puddles of water by accident. Therefore, my outdoor activities during those three months were significantly limited.

During the summer of 1997, as we were getting ready for the rainy season, we had an unexpected surprise – the septic system at my parents' house collapsed creating an uninhabitable environment. I called my dad in the United States to give him this horrible news. His reaction was obviously shock and frustration. What did you guys do? When did this happen? Was anyone hurt? Everything was fine except the fact that we would not be able to use the bathroom for a while.

I was raised in an environment which typically relies on family members abroad for financial support. It is the "foreign travelers," as they are commonly referred to, who would meet the most basic needs of the family, such as, food, clothes, housing and educational expenses. But more than just simply meeting the basic needs of their immediate family, these individuals are responsible for the well-being of their extended families as well.

My father had two sisters and one brother, who have a combined total of 33 children. While my father was not fully responsible for feeding my cousins, their educational expenses however, fell solely on his shoulders. The summer season was the time of the year when he would save up money so he could pay his children's school fees as well as the fees for his nieces and nephews. The collapse of our septic system could not have happened at a worse time.

I am the fourth child on my mother's side and the fifth on my father's side. The community I grew up in is a male dominant society, which makes masculinity part of growing up fast. My oldest brother had left for the United States the year before, and my older half-brother was living in Mali at the time. Mali is about an hour flight from The Gambia. Also, four of my older cousins were living with us. However, despite the fact that these guys were much older than me and had more experience in business transactions, my father decided to put me in charge of the project of rebuilding the septic system.

This was a huge undertaking at the time for me. Although I'd always been business savvy prior to this event, I had never imagined tackling such a problem at that early age. The overall project cost about $3000 (USD), which amounted to D33000 (Gambian dalasi). I hired the contractors, bought the materials, and came up with the plan of action. The entire project lasted less than a month, and our residential compound was back to normal. My father was very impressed with my ability to undertake this huge project and bring it to a successful completion, but the "Aha" moment for my father, was when I returned him the $200 that was left. "For the first time, someone has been fully forthcoming with me regarding money," said my father. This has led my father to believe in me more than anyone else. I fully became his "right-hand."

From that moment on, I was in charge of running the day to day financial operation of our household, from buying groceries to distributing money among my stepmother and my mother. This was important since my father would only visit once a year for about two months. By the end of that year, my father was so impressed with my performance that he thought, if I could attend to and run a 26 person household and manage his finances while in The Gambia, imagine what I could do if I was living in the United States? He decided to apply for a U.S. visa for me at the end of 1997, but it was denied without any definitive explanation as to why. Although that was disappointing, it was the right thing for me. Things I would later face in the U.S. would have been almost impossible to endure at that age.

The Journey to America

Three years later, on July 26th, 2000. I was finally granted a U.S. visa. My father had visited home that summer during the issuance of the visa and we celebrated this major milestone. I just completed my eighth grade and would normally have been getting ready for the summer vacation. Instead, I was embarking on a journey known to only those who have undergone the experience. My family and friends all envied me and could only wish to have a similar opportunity.

As I was getting ready to journey to the United States, I was excited, nervous, curious and anxious. The movies we saw back home glamorized the United States in a manner that is very enticing and appealing. We all wish we could be living in such an amazing place. I began to imagine what kind of car I would be driving; what kind of house I would be living in; how awesome the schools would be as compared to the "run-down" buildings I went to school in and so on. We were all thrilled beyond words that I would have the chance to go to a place of abundant opportunity for all who look for it. All these thoughts kept me up a lot of nights that summer.

While I was having my fantasies, my family was struggling to buy my ticket to come to the States. Since this was the responsibility of my father, it would not have been a problem if he was in the United States. But staying in The Gambia at the time made it difficult for him to acquire the money. It took a month and half for me to finally get a ticket to come to the United States.

On Saturday, September 2nd, 2000, my father's good friend who lives in New York, and whom my father had been asking for help called and said he bought the ticket. "When will he be leaving?" my father asked. "Tomorrow morning." On the one hand, my father was relieved that I could finally leave, but on the other hand, it was beyond belief that I would be leaving my community, friends and family the very next day.

How can you embark on a journey to a country you have never been to without any real preparation? Well, that's what you call life. With no money, with no real place to stay, I was preparing to leave for a new land; a land so glamorous, only the most fortunate are blessed to experience it.

Now was my turn. Reality was seeping in, rushing in like a torrent of rain. The night before my departure, we all stayed up into the wee hours of the morning. Where once pure ecstasy pervaded my every moment that summer, mixed emotions erupted that night as me, my mother, grandmother and my siblings shared one last night together. They admonished me on the enormity of my responsibility to them, to the survival of the family, and not to forget my roots and the meaning of family and the future lying ahead of me.

My grandmother repeated what she had recited so often to me as I sat in her lap as a young boy, "You can only know where you're going if you know where you came from!" In the same breath, she helped me to put the future and the past into some context. She referred to the analogy that the rearview mirror is much smaller than the windshield on a car, reminding me that what is before me is more important than what is behind me. That while I needed to be mindful of the past, if I dwelt too much on it, I would be taking my eyes off the road in front of me and could crash into a heap of personal destruction.

But while we were bathing in the warmth of great expectations and personal obligation, the women in my life were racked with feelings of sadness and ambivalence. More than anyone else, my grandmother knew my visual impairment was very serious and she initially was opposed to sending me off to America at such a young age, with such a serious disability. She was my constant companion, as I was hers, since I was homebound by my advancing blindness. She was my best buddy. She alone understood the extent of my sightlessness, while others only sensed I couldn't see well.

Even my father, who left The Gambia when I was only two years old, didn't fully grasp the enormity of my visual ailment. In any event, he knew America would be better for me: better doctors, more light, more resources and greater chances to improve one's condition. He knew what my mother and grandmother did not know for they had never experienced the miracle of America.

They worried that last night, as they wept. We all wept. We were all nervous. Even I, after weeks of great anticipation and excitement, was overcome with buyer's remorse as the imminence of my departure cropped up so suddenly. I would be leaving my family, my small town, everything I had known, the familiarity of my surroundings and the loving embrace of a tight knit family and women who adored me and protected me every moment of everyday of my life. The very next day!

But the existential reality trumped our emotional ambivalence. The financial situation we were in dictated that I would have to go in order to earn money and send it home. Money I could only earn in America. These two realities – economic necessity and emotional attachment – caused us great turmoil that night, but we didn't hesitate to change the course of events because we simply did not have the luxury of choice.

~

After a short slumber, we awoke in the early morning for my last breakfast at home. My mother cooked the tradition meal of porridge and milk, and we drank it together. All of my family and all of the neighbors joined us for morning prayers. This was a big deal, and all eyes were on me that morning.

I packed a small suitcase with very few items: two pants and two shirts, a few pieces of African attire, but not much more. It didn't make sense to take clothes to America, when they were needed home in The Gambia. Visitors to Africa and many parts of the Third World rarely return with clothing and other personal items far more valuable to the hosts.

Aside from those few items, my grandmother gave me her favorite prayer mat, one she used only twice a year during two of the biggest religious holidays celebrated by Muslims worldwide: Eid-Ul-Fitr (the festival of breaking of the fast after the Holy month of Ramadan) and Eid-Al-Adha (the festival of the sacrifice). She gave me this cherished possession as a reminder to remember my faith and traditions. Don't forget who you are. Don't forget where you came from. Don't forget your people, your history and legacy. It was at that moment that I began to understand the power of my religious faith, as I was leaving its sanctuary. Until then, religion was like water to a fish for me. And a fish doesn't know he's wet until he's dry, until he has left the water he was born into. So I became aware of my Muslim identity, as I was leaving home.

I stepped out of the house at about nine o'clock to leave into an uncertain future; I looked back at my mother and grandmother weeping, my heart swelling in a menagerie of emotion I can hardly describe. They couldn't stand to accompany me to the airport, so my father drove me and my siblings to The Gambia International Airport. Though we were in the rainy season, the sun was shining brightly the day of my departure. Arriving at the airport, my father came across some other Gambians headed to America and asked them to look after me on the long journey.

I boarded an Air Afrique plane at 11 that morning, the first plane I'd been on in my life. I don't remember looking down at my homeland as the plane soared into the air because I was overcome with emotion, my eyes streaming tears. "Oh my God! I am leaving!" While I had no idea what to expect in the U.S., the regret of leaving my family led me to utter these words, "I'll not fail in the United States."

It was a short 25 minute flight to Senegal, where I would change planes. There was a three and a half hour layover there where I waited alone; nothing to eat. The plane departed Senegal at 4 PM and flew eight and a half hours over the vast Atlantic Ocean to JFK airport in New York.

At 9:53 pm on Sunday, September 3rd 2000, my plane landed at the John F. Kennedy International Airport. As the plane was getting ready to land, circling through the beautiful skies over New York City, I could not help but smile. Seeing the brighter lights gave me a glimmer of hope about my new life. A hope that I would be able to go out at night without fear; a hope that I would be able to drive because my vision would be restored; a hope that I would be able to finally enjoy life because I was now in a country where any dream is possible and where imaginations could turn into creations.

This idea about the land of the free and of opportunity is what made the United States what it is today; the belief that anyone can make it in this great nation if you're willing to try. Anyone with a compelling vision and an unshakable desire should be able to thrive. But more importantly, all these great manifestation of worldly realities about the United States comes down to one word...decision. Our lives are controlled by the decisions we make.

As I got off the plane and headed towards immigration, I was overcome with joy and it felt surreal that I was actually in the United States. My first major highlight was the escalator as I stood there contemplating whether to take the regular stairs or the "automatic stairs" (which I'd never seen before). I joined a couple of other newcomers gawking at the mechanical miracle. After a few moments, we all decided to take the regular stairs just to be "safe."

After clearing Immigration and Customs, I ventured through the airport in complete amazement. Though it was nighttime, everything was so brightly lit. I could finally see for the first time at night; and for the first time since I was four years old, I wasn't afraid of being outside at night. For the first time, I felt confident again. I felt at peace with myself, thinking that finally, I would be able to enjoy my life. The bright lights at the Kennedy Airport gave me hope for a new beginning: a beginning that would be unlike any in the previous 16 years of my life. At the very least, I would be able to engage in activities I restrained myself from doing after sunset.

I walked to the arrival lobby where I saw my brother in his bright red shirt, smiling from ear to ear. I hadn't seen him since he left The Gambia four years earlier, when I was just twelve. He was amazed by my size for I had grown up considerably since we were last together. He was looking sharp. He had the look of "America" as we usually refer to it in The Gambia. We rode in his brand new green Subaru Outback. As we pulled from the parking lot on the fourth floor, my first question was, "You parked on the fourth floor?" I looked confused, and was wondering how in the world are we going to get down? As he looked at the shock on my face, he started laughing and said, "Young man, welcome to the United States."

My brother lives in Poughkeepsie, which is about 75 miles north of New York City. A typical drive would take about an hour and half. Unfortunately, it took us five hours to reach our destination, not because of New York's crazy traffic or, for that matter, encountering an accident, but that we were lost. This was the era before GPS became prevalent. After lots of stops along the way asking for directions, we finally got home around 4 a.m. Strangely, it took nearly as long to cross the Atlantic as it did for us to drive less than 100 miles to his apartment. Journeys are always unpredictable, as I have come to learn.

By the time we got home, some of my fears began to resurface. The further away we got from New York City, the fewer the bright lights. It began to seem that not everything was as glamorous as I thought. The excitement that I enjoyed a few moments ago about my future began to fade away. My old negative thoughts of inferiority and the inability to attain a brighter future began to emerge again.

I was in such an emotional whirlwind that I forgot how hungry I had become, having not eaten much since that morning's porridge. My brother stopped to buy my first meal in America: a sandwich and soda from McDonalds. It was awesome. How appropriate!

We arrived at my brother's apartment complex in the middle of the night, after nearly 24 hours of travel. It was dark. I was once again blind. My brother guided me through the dark to his one-bedroom apartment, which he shared with his wife and her eight year old son. He was not quite aware of the extent of my sightlessness, as he had left The Gambia when I was much younger and my sight much better. I was relieved by the light illuminating the apartment. I could see again.

Since they had not expected me so soon, they had not prepared a place for me to sleep. So I slept on a mattress in the living room. That night, as I lay my head on the pillow, in the dark, in this new place, in this new country, my thoughts flooded over me. As I dozed off to sleep, I thought, "This is it?" "This was all?" No gold studded streets, no Hollywood sets, no glamorous home, no fantasy unfurled. Such is the experience of many immigrants I have come to learn: the shocking realization that our expectations were far grander than reality could ever allow. I slept soundly as my mind wandered and wondered what the next day would bring.

~

The next morning, I woke up very early (my brother had to go to work) to a bright, beautiful and chilly morning full of excitement and anxiety: excitement, because I was about to experience a lifestyle that I envisioned from movies for years. The idea that I would be going to school in a car instead of walking to the main highway to wait for the bus was an exhilarating experience.

The day started with a pancake breakfast, which was quite interesting because having pancakes for breakfast did seem a little weird to me. In The Gambia, we only ate pancakes during certain occasions, such as naming ceremonies, weddings and birthday parties. I asked, instead, for Corn Flakes which, unlike here in America, was a luxury item for my family in The Gambia. There you could only buy Corn Flakes at the supermarket, which seemed to be only reserved for the wealthy people. To me, this was a big deal, which my brother – now comfortable in America – had obviously forgotten.

My breakfast choice was a bit disappointing for my brother because he spent a lot of time making the pancakes for me. I would later become a huge fan of pancakes after discovering the distinctions between The Gambian Pancake and American flapjacks.

Leaving the apartment that second day, I was astonished by the lush lawns in the apartment complex. This was new to me, for in The Gambia, lawns were rare, and sandy roads were the rule, except for the homes of the upper class. So many contrasts. So much to learn.

~

A lot of thoughts came to me as we were driving to school for registration: what the buildings would look like, how the students would be dressed since the students in American movies don't wear uniforms, but more importantly, how I would be received? Those thoughts quickly manifested into reality because I was now able to witness the reality of being a student in the United States.

On our way back from school registration, my brother asked if I was hungry. While I was not all that hungry, I could not wait to start munching on all those delicious dishes that I've been longing for so long.

"Yes, I am hungry."

"What would you like to eat?" he asked

Without hesitation, I replied, "Chicken.".

"What kind?" he asked.

I was quiet for a moment thinking, what does he mean by what kind? In my world, chicken is chicken.

"Any kind of chicken would be fine." (In my head I was thinking that as long as it's chicken, I'm good).

"Alright young man, let's head to KFC."

So my second major meal in the U.S., after being welcomed with a McDonald's sandwich the night before, happened to be a 12 piece bucket of fried chicken. As we stopped at the first post of the drive thru, my brother said, "Could we get 12 piece fried chicken, corn and mashed potato." At this point, all I was thinking was when are we going to get out of the car to walk into this place so I can get my chicken. Therefore, I was stunned when the order was handed to us. As my brother drove away he handed me this huge bucket of chicken. "That's all yours boy." "Really?" I asked. With an amusing smile, he said, "Yes."

With no one to worry about sharing, with no group of people rushing through the meal and with no worries about sharing the last tiny piece of chicken, I just giggled and said out loud, "God bless America." This was the beginning of abundant thinking and the eradication of scarcity mentality.

I was placed in 11th grade since I was 16 years old and "had enough credits to skip grade 9 and 10," according to my Guidance Counselor. This was a defining moment for me. If I was placed in 9th grade as I was supposed to be, then I probably would not have had a high school diploma because my experience at Poughkeepsie was excruciating and tormenting. At Poughkeepsie High School, I didn't have a social support group among my peers. I did not have friends or anyone to socialize with.

My first big challenge at Poughkeepsie High School was the misconceptions and misinformation about Africa. The first question I was asked by a student at the school was about which airport I flew in from. "How was the flight from Johannesburg?" Despite the ignorance of the student's question, I was equally ignorant. "Where is that?" "What do you mean?" I asked. "I mean Johannesburg." he responded. After looking at him confused for the second time, he asked, "Isn't Johannesburg the only airport in Africa?" Oh, I finally got it. Johannesburg is actually a city somewhere in Africa. "No, I came from Banjul International Airport." Now, he looked really confused. He said, "What the f**k is this n****r talking about?" I was so excited to hear those words because I'd heard words like this in American movies before. So, now it felt like I was living in America. The resemblance to the movies was beginning to surface. But beside that, what was truly beginning to surface in this conversation was the collision between ignorance and stupidity. As Martin Luther King Jr. put it, "Nothing in all the world is more dangerous than sincere ignorance and conscientious stupidity."

Growing up in The Gambia, I never consciously identified as African. But my conversation with that student my first day of school marked the beginning of me seeing myself not as a Gambian, but rather, as a representative of a continent that has over 54 countries, over 1500 different languages, and over a thousand beliefs, cultures and values. This new identity that was given to me by my new American classmates has made me grow up much faster than expected. Whenever there was a conversation about Africa, I was the one they would refer to for ideas, never mind that my knowledge and understanding of Africa ceased within the sub-region of West Africa.

While the initial question of Johannesburg being the only airport in Africa was shocking, it was no match to a question that followed from another student. In her genuine and soft spoken voice, she asked: "Just out of curiosity, do ya wear clothes in Africa?" I was at first speechless, but slowly I could feel the anger building up in me. As she looked in my face, with my eyes turning red and my face looking like I was about to punch somebody in the face, she quickly replied: "I didn't mean no offense." While I could not have the proper words to respond to her, I began to wake up to a new reality of life.

I was living in an environment that has, as the great Nigerian writer Chimamanda Adichie calls it, "the single story" about Africa. In this single story, my classmates' view of Africa has been a place full of disease, wildlife, war, poverty, and incomprehensible people with no sense of civilization. Living in America for quite some time now, I now understand my classmates' questions and ignorance of Africa. While I could call these silly questions or stereotypes of Africa, I don't think that would be the correct explanation. The assumptions that my classmates had of Africa were not based on their own knowledge or facts. They made a conclusive judgment about what Africa represents without any evidence. That is more than stereotyping in itself; it is a dangerous approach towards life.

Even though I could not understand my classmates' attitude about Africa based on the little information they knew of it, the teachers' attitudes surprised me the most. In general, I was always quiet in public settings, especially in the classroom, for reasons that are sometimes beyond my control. But as an educator now, I would think that a teacher would inquire about his/her student's competence based on reliable sources prior to making a judgment about the student's understanding capacity.

Instead of this approach, on my second day, one of my teachers, whose class I don't remember because of the short time I spent in there, stated to me that I would be transferred to a reading class since I came from a French speaking country. "I am not from a French-speaking country," I replied. "What is the official language of your native country?" "English," I replied. In a surprised voice, she said, "Really?" To which I responded "yes." Anyway, you would need to go to the reading class to improve your skills."

What really surprised me was that despite not knowing anything about me, she had already concluded that I was not capable of being in her class. But more importantly, she had already categorized me as incompetent simply because of who I was. I am not saying that she didn't think highly of Africans, but rather, like my fellow students, this teacher was simply clueless about Africa. One thing I did admire about this conversation, however, was the professionalism and respectful manner of her request.

The most stunning, incomprehensible, and out of the ordinary comment actually came not from a student or a teacher who might be ignorant about Africa, but rather, from my history teacher who should, one would think, have had understanding and tolerance due to his presumed understanding of past events. As a history teacher, I define history as: To know the past, so we can understand the present, and be therefore able to predict future events. But I am not ignorant enough to imply that because someone knows something, they necessarily understand or sympathize with it.

I came to class one day wearing my beautiful African attire. This was not necessarily planned, because, since I live in America, I should dress like an American, so I thought. But I ran out of clean clothes that day. Every class I attended that morning, all the teachers complimented me as to how beautiful my clothing was. For a second, I thought, it was not harmful to wear African clothes in America. Just like most things in life, there are exceptions to every rule. My morning class teachers were the norm in this case, but I was about to encounter the exception.

I walked into my history class all confident and looking forward to another compliment. As I walked in, my teacher was standing at his podium, looking grumpy and staring at me from top to bottom as if I told him the most horrifying news of his life. He started his class as usual. The only thing unusual was how he was looking at me. A few minutes after class started, as he continued to speak, he couldn't take it anymore, he all of sudden said, "If people want to wear their funny dresses, they should stay in their country. This is America."

If only I could fast forward to today, my response would have been much different now that I know my rights and responsibilities. Instead, I started shaking and put my head down. The same way that I was surprised, my classmates were equally astonished, but, for whatever reason, no one said a word about it. The class just proceeded as normal. Looking back, I always ask myself, why didn't anyone say anything? The only reason I can think of now is maybe because I had no friends in the room. While the class continued, I did not continue as usual ever since that day. That was the last time I ever wore my African attire with the exception of Eid-Al-

Fitr and Eid-Al-Adha. But due to the memories from those comments, I always took off those clothes as soon as we came from the prayer place.

"Try to understand men. If you understand each other, you will be kind to each other. Knowing a man well never leads to hate and almost always leads to love" (John Steinbeck). I wonder how the world would be if we all lived by this principle? Well, one thing is for sure, the world would be more peaceful, tolerant, and understanding. Most of the challenges of the world today come from the absence of our common bond of humanity. Our lives today are typically based on the idea of *us and them*. This sort of thinking creates hatred and conflict. There is more to life than this kind of thinking. We were never created to live *just a life*; we were made to contribute in making a difference in not just the lives of the few people around us, but in the lives of as many people as possible. And the biggest gift we can give to everyone who we come in contact with is to give our unconditional love, tolerance and appreciation.

In every despair, regardless of how dire the situation might be, there is always goodness within. While my experience at Poughkeepsie High School was grim, one person turned everything around for me for the better. Remember the teacher who told me I need to be transferred to a reading class since I came from a "French speaking country?" What I did not realize at the time was that she was actually being directed by God. Looking back now, I realized nothing in this world happens by accident. All things happen for a specific reason and we usually think our problems and enemies are here to defeat us. Instead, what if we ask this question anytime we face a challenge: how can I use this situation to help me grow or strengthen my character?

As soon as I walked into my reading class, the teacher had this big smile on her face as if she just received the gift of a lifetime. I felt so relieved and right away I knew this was the right place for me, "HOW ARE YOU DOING?" she said, I responded in my usual Gambian way, "Fine." She looked at my schedule and, to my surprise and delight, pronounced my name perfectly. I sat down looking at everyone, waiting for those agonizing questions of: where are you from? What is life in Africa like? Or, the silly questions I encountered earlier. Instead, this awesome teacher, Ms. Felter said, "Class, can we introduce ourselves to Alhassan?"

Rather than feeling like an outsider, the idea of others introducing themselves to me made me feel comfortable when it was my turn to speak. It felt like a safe environment with tremendous love and laughter. Ms. Felter was always full of energy and had a positive attitude every single day.

What I found in Ms. Felter's class is what I now call, "steps of faith." Nothing in this world happens by accident. Rather, everything that occurs in our lives is helping to propel us to the next level. At the beginning, it wouldn't seem like those situations arise to increase us to our next level, but in reality, they are. I would probably not have gotten a high school diploma if I wasn't transferred to Ms. Felter's class. This was the only place in the school where I could be myself and not be laughed at or judged. The class comprised of newly arrived students from all over the world, mostly from Latin America. Since I was the only African in the school, these "immigrants" became my friends. We later called the class "United Nations."

Ms. Felter's room provided more than just dignity and comfort for me, it provided basic essential needs of all human beings. Among these are food, love, compassion and strength. There were many occasions in which I came to school without breakfast and since I was not eligible for free lunch because "my household income exceeds the limits for free lunch," I could not eat in the cafeteria without paying for it. While I never told Ms. Felter about my living condition or, for that matter, starvation at school, she nevertheless would provide hot chocolate and crackers when I showed up to her class before school started.

This simple act of generosity made it easier for me to get through high school. While she was not aware of this, the food she fed me would some days be my only meal of the day. Besides feeding me and other students, Ms. Felter also had a stack of clothes in her closet. She would always pay attention to what students in the class were wearing. When she noticed a pattern of a student wearing the same clothes most of the time, she would bring that student in the closet and say "I went shopping this weekend, but I happened to buy more than I need, check these out and see if you would like any of them and take as much as you want." This sort of statement made me feel special rather than feeling like it's charity or that she felt sorry for me.

Prejudice, is the single biggest danger to peace and stability in all four corners of the globe. Prejudice creates a sense of "us" vs. "them." It eradicates the dignity in humanity. Furthermore, it creates a false sense of superiority over others. Prejudice implies that the "other" is not fully equal to you. It is this false sense of entitlement that creates most of today's world conflicts. Prejudice is the means by which people judge others, not necessarily based on facts, but rather based on our preconceived notion of that person or place. It is typically drawn from our values, beliefs or cultural understanding.

A few months after my history teacher's appalling comments about my choice of clothing, he began to know me better. We developed a strong relationship based on understanding each other's background and values. I would go to him during lunch, when all the students would be in the cafeteria, and ask him for help since I literally knew nothing about U.S. history prior to coming to America. I still remember creating a buzz in the classroom when I raised my hand and asked, "Who is George Washington?" This was a sign that I needed to work harder than anyone in that class. Regardless of how much a teacher might despise a student, as long as that student shows consistent effort and a desire to succeed, s/he will eventually be at least tolerated by that teacher. At least, that's what I believed happened between me and my history teacher.

During our lunch sessions of tutoring support, I began to understand why my history teacher would make such a statement about my choice of clothing. He had distaste for anything that was not associated with America. He had a great pride in what it meant to be an American and unfortunately, had a very narrow view of what it meant to respect America and be proud of it.

For instance, he believed that English should be the only language spoken in this country. No other dress except those that are worn by most people should be worn in society. After several conversations, he began to understand my story and who I was as a person rather than what he perceived me to be (which was another immigrant reaping the benefits of America and not being appreciative of it). As he began to internalize my story, he began to look more into the immigrant issue, which he found to be intriguing.   Thus, our final class project became interviewing an immigrant and writing about their experience in America.   This became a very exciting experience for me and my classmates and the results were emotionally surprising.

By the end of the project, as we read these stories out loud, we decided as a class that we would put these stories in a book so that the rest of our community could learn about their neighbors, coworkers, and fellow students whom they tended to consider as "them," rather than attaining a real understanding of that person. The publication of *Poughkeepsie Pride: The Stories of our Immigrants* became one of the most exciting and memorable days of my high school experience and perhaps one of the most meaningful projects for my classmates as well.

PART III

Where there is love, there is no darkness

--Burundian Proverb

Meeting Steward Pickett

The people that are put in your life are not there by accident. Love them, cherish them and be grateful for their presence. These individuals were purposefully chosen to be part of your life to help you get to the next level. One of those individuals for me happens to be Dr. Steward Pickett. Steward is my brother's best friend. They had met about a year before I arrived in the United States. My father and brother were performing West African music associated with the griot traditions. They both played the Kora, a Mandinka long-necked harp built from a large calabash cut in half and covered with cow skin.

My father and brother – the two griots -- were performing at a cultural arts event attended by Dr. Steward Pickett, a prominent researcher in the field of plant ecology. He was impressed and sought them out after the performance. He eventually invited my brother to dinner to learn more about our griot culture and community. They became close friends.

It was no surprise then when my brother took me to visit Dr. Pickett very soon after I arrived in America. I was introduced to Steward on Friday, September 8th, 2000, five days after my arrival in the U.S. We were invited to dinner at his house where he made us a nice Moroccan Lamb Tagine.

I was very impressed with his house, a 19th century Victorian house with a long driveway and a huge front and backyard. This was impressive to me because all I had seen since my arrival in Poughkeepsie were apartment buildings which were usually congested. This home was grand. Outside, the home was skirted with a proud and well-manicured lawn, a symbol of wealth in my verdant homeland. His home was adorned with artworks from around the world and fine furniture, rugs and fancy fixtures at every corner. He lived alone in what I could imagine was a mansion, the first I had ever encountered.

My eyes widened at the sight of all the beautifully bound books. Was this a library, I thought to myself. Surely, this was the home of a wealthy man, an intelligent man, and a man with a heart as big and as impressive as his home.

We spent about four hours with Steward and then my brother mentioned to him about my inability to see at night and that we were in the process of looking for an eye doctor who could evaluate me and hopefully finally come up with a diagnosis for this grueling problem. My brother explained that I had never been diagnosed by a doctor and my vision ailment was worsening as I grew into manhood.

Very casually, Steward suggested that we see his doctor. We, of course were flattered, but demurred, explaining that we hadn't yet obtained medical insurance. Steward, ever so magnanimously, insisted that we shouldn't wait, especially since my vision problems would hamper my education. We agreed to accept his generosity, the first of many gestures of kindness and compassion he would show us in the years to come.

On September 26, I went with Steward for an eye exam. How do I still remember that date? Well, it's simple. It's a date carved into my psyche. This date marked the beginning of a new chapter in my life, a chapter that would bring me to making another conscious decision about my path forward. This date became a turning point in the direction of my future. Up to this point, my impression was that my life had been shaped by my condition. My belief was that the conditions of my life defined my future. But actually, looking back now, it was the decisions I made that shaped the direction of my future.

Each and every single day, we all make dozens, if not hundreds of decisions that consciously or subconsciously are shaping the course of our lives. Sometimes we believe that our biography is the force that shapes our destiny. While this might be true in the sense that your belief system may become your reality, biography is the furthest thing from destiny. It is our decisions that mold the trajectory of our lives.

~

On our way to the eye doctor's office, I was overwhelmed with joy, but at the same time, anxious. Overwhelmed with joy, because it was possible I would finally be able to see at night and begin to live a "normal" life. Anxious, because I was not sure what to expect. What if the doctor said that my condition was incurable? What if the procedure had complications? All of these ideas were playing in my head as we were heading to the doctor's office. Steward was both entertaining and hospitable. He is the most thoughtful person I've known my entire life. What I admire most about Steward is his questioning technique, which is always intriguing. He engaged me in conversations about The Gambia and my thoughts about the U.S. so far.

At around 4:45 p.m. we pulled into the doctor's parking lot, facing a large red brick building. My first observation was how different the clinic was compared to the hospital I visited in The Gambia. The floor was spotless, with a good scent and slow jazz music playing in the background. I couldn't believe that I was in a doctor's office. But more importantly, I could not believe how pleasant the receptionist and the staff members were in this clinic.

I grew up in an environment where healthcare practitioners usually felt like they were doing you a favor whenever they engaged with you. My experience with those healthcare professionals had been so unpleasant that I still can vividly remember the harsh tone with which the eye doctor asked "What do you mean you can't see at night?" The idea of patient or customer satisfaction was usually absent in the dialogue.

As we sat in the waiting room enjoying the jazz music, this tall man walked in with a clipboard with my file. "You must be Las. Hi, I am Dr. Lance. Come on in." At this point, I didn't know what to feel, but one thing I do remember was how frightened I was. All I was hoping was not to get any bad news about my condition. After several hours of questioning, testing and eye dilation, we were finally called back in for our final conversation with the doctor. "Steward, based on the initial result of the examination, Las has Stargardt. It is a rare vision condition that occurs in children and it would gradually degrade the quality of the vision over time."

According to the American Macular Degeneration Foundation (AMDF), Stargardt is a rare macular degeneration disease that occurs in one in 20,000 children and teenagers. Stargardt disease was named after Karl Stargardt, German ophthalmologist who first reported a case in his practice in 1901.

Stargardt affects both eyes, and develops sometime between the ages of six and twenty, when kids notice difficulties in reading or adapting to bright light. The cause and treatments of the disease in young people are different from those of age-related macular degeneration. Stargardt disease is the result of a gene called ABCA4 and is usually a recessive trait. When both parents carry the ABCA4 mutation, there is a 25 percent chance their children will have Stargardt disease.

In other words, I inherited this horrible defect, along with all of the wonderful traits handed down to me, generation to generation, father to son: including the proud tradition of the griot, the rich African heritage and the profound devotion to the Creator of the universe. My eyes were an heirloom, bequeathed to me, an inheritance I had no choice but to accept, an inheritance I would one day come to appreciate rather than curse. This black hole was growing on the rear of my eyeball, like a spot eclipsing my sight from the center out to the edges of my peripheral vision. Though I had not experienced pitch black blindness, I was experiencing the slow and steady deterioration of my eyesight, just as I was growing into a man.

While I had no clue as to what Stargardt meant or its effect, one thing clearly stood out to me. "With this condition, it's very likely that Las could be legally blind in a decade." I was sixteen years old at that point; doing the math, I could be legally blind by the age of 26. "However," Dr. Lance continued, "you need to see a retinal specialist for further testing to come to a more authentic conclusion."

Whether a further test was needed or not did not matter to me at that point. All I could think of, or worry about, was the fact that I could be legally blind by the age of 26. Words could not begin to describe how I felt when I heard those words. It made me think of the old saying, "what you don't know doesn't hurt you." At that particular moment, I was thinking why I even came for the eye evaluation.

While I was thrilled and anxious on our way to the doctor's office, I was quiet and sad on the way back. Despite Steward's unique conversational skills, he could not get me engaged in a conversation. What I was thinking about was that I had a life without a future. Who'd marry a blind person? Who would give me a job? What's the point of even furthering my education, if my final activities would stop at the age of 26? How would I ever fight for the rights of the least fortunate members of society? This had been a passion of mine since childhood.

These were not crazy ideas, but a reflection of the environment in which I grew up. If I were to spend the rest of my life in The Gambia and this prognosis would have come true, these thoughts would have been my reality. While it may sound like a crazy idea for the moment, it was nevertheless, reflective of the mistreatment of people with disabilities in The Gambia at the time. Instead of focusing on what other capabilities a disabled person might have, we tended to focus solely on their disability and make that the definitive story of their life rather than focusing on what they could contribute to humanity.

Steward took me to a really great Mexican restaurant in an attempt to make me feel good or at least take my mind off the issue for a moment. As much as I liked Mexican food, nothing on that day could make me feel good or, make me forgo the thoughts of the diagnosis. As we began to have a conversation, Steward focused on how school was going for me. As much as I liked to talk about education and the exchange of ideas about various topics and my classmates, that day was just not the right day for any sort of conversation. As I began to give responses, such as "good" and "alright" to every question, Steward quickly realized that I needed some time alone. At home that night, there was nothing I could do but to cry myself to sleep.

~

I contacted my mom and grandmother the next day to give them the doctor's report. As you can imagine, even though they knew something was wrong with my sight, they never envisioned to hear the news that I might potentially be legally blind by the age of 26. "Namie, I might be blind by the age of 26 according to the eye doctor." After a short pause, she replied, "That's what they said, but that's not what God said." This was not a surprise coming from my grandma. She was the most spiritual human being that I ever came across in my life. Her biggest focus had always been to find meaning, even under the most difficult of circumstances.

Namie always said, "Life is nothing but a journey. Even the longest is short. This life is more like a rest stop on a highway." I had heard these words for years growing up, but, when you hear something for so long, you become immune to it. I never paid full attention to the meaning behind those words. But looking back now, they have become my guiding principle. The analogy of life being like a rest stop is fascinating to me now.

As my conversation with my grandmother continued, she began to explain that I would fulfill my God-given destiny, whatever that may be. "You were born with the tools necessary to fulfill your destiny. God did not make a mistake in creating you in such a condition." It was at this point that I began to have a little comfort knowing that God's plans, regardless of how much we may not prefer them at the moment, are always best for us. I began to think that even though I might not understand the reason(s) why this happened to me, I nevertheless knew that it's possible that it might be to serve a greater purpose. However, this did not fully convince me that I would be fine; it only took me off that state of misery for a moment.

My conversation with my mom was slightly different from that of my Grandmother. My mother is a straight shooter who does not sugarcoat her feelings and is not as deeply inspirational as my grandmother. Her first response was, "They're lying. You are fine. You've lived your entire life with this condition. How could they predict that you might be blind in the future?" It was slightly difficult to have a conversation with Mom because she is not the most patient person. She always jumps to conclusions without fully grasping the information presented. Thus, the phone call ended without me having any comfort.

~

I began a new chapter in my life the next day: a chapter of uncertainty, constant worry, and fear. As I went to school that Monday, all that was in the back of my mind was "Why even bother?" This phrase had defined who I became and what I did for a long time. Anytime I attempted to do something great, all I would say to myself was, why bother if I only have certain years to live a meaningful life. I associated blindness with my life: not that I would attempt suicide. Culturally, that was not part of our vocabulary, so thoughts as such never came to my mind. But I always discouraged myself from moving forward on virtually anything significant because I thought that my achievements would be short lived, since I might not be able to meaningfully live the life I desired.

Three weeks after my initial visit to Dr. Lance's office, I went to see a retinal specialist who was supposed to confirm the initial diagnosis. On this day, I was extremely paranoid, but at the same time, slightly hopeful that Dr. Lance misdiagnosed me. The visit to Dr. Johnson's office ended up being one of my shortest doctor visits ever. Dr. Johnson was not as friendly as Dr. Lance. He walked into the room and was ready for business. "You are diagnosed with having Stargardt, and are here for confirmation?" Within a matter of five minutes of examination, he called in his assistant. "He has Stargardt. Please refer him to Lighthouse International." All he said to me was "Take care, and best of luck to you."

~

Lighthouse International is an organization dedicated to the prevention, treatment and empowerment of people with vision loss. They enhance the experience of people with low vision through in-home care. The day I was visited by a specialist from Lighthouse was another grim day of my life. The specialist who came to my home to assess my situation was Wendy. She began by explaining to me the process of homecare. The main services that would be provided to me, if needed, were cooking, laundry, shopping and any other household chores. The idea of fully going blind began to take root in my mind. "It looks like you're fine for now, so we'll check-in with you every two years," Wendy told me. I was devastated when Wendy left. I began to cry uncontrollably, and all sorts of negative unimaginable questions came to me about my future -- the biggest one being, why me?

While I cannot control the events of my life, I do have control over how I feel. The only problem was that I didn't know this back in those days. This idea that we cannot control the events, but we're 100% in control of how we feel about that particular issue or event became the driving force of my classroom norms today. I had chosen to give myself a badge of worthlessness due to something that was beyond my control. I thought that the only means upon which I could live a productive and successful life was to have all areas of my life functioning the way they should. Sadly though, I've lived most of my life with that impression.

~

I continued to live my life normally, to the best of my ability, with my brother and his wife. As you can imagine, that first year in the States was an immense challenge. I was having a difficult time at school. I could barely see the board. I could barely understand the words my teachers were saying.

After school, I worked every evening until 10 at night, home by 11, with little or no time to study, a short slumber and back to school by 7:40 the next morning. I was perpetually exhausted, often late to my first period class, math, which I had never excelled in. Add a language barrier to my constant fatigue, lack of focus, anemic grades and you get a struggling student, often on the verge of dropping out completely.

Home life was equally a struggle. My presence – growing young man – squeezed into a one bedroom apartment with a husband and wife (not long married), and her eight year old son, put enormous pressure on the couple. She was American born, unaccustomed to the traditions of our native continent and she could not understand why my brother had no choice but to invite me into his home. I think she may have resented my intrusion, justifiably so, I must confess.

And my father would just show up any time without notice, knocking on the door. This was so African and so foreign to my brother's American wife, who thought the entire situation was just rude. And while I might not disagree with her, we were simply following our cultural genetic code, hard wired for generations. You simply could not turn your back on a family member. No matter what!

Before the end of my junior year, at the age of 17, my brother and his wife began to move on with their lives, and so did I. First, she moved out, forcing my brother to split his time between the two residences. Eventually, that arrangement wore thin and they parted ways completely. This put tremendous pressure on my brother, who was a student and a working teacher with limited financial resources. We would be evicted before long, just one month before the end of my junior year. I would need to find another place to stay. I had been in America less than one year. With nowhere to turn, I moved in with Steward the last month of the school year, June, but I would have to find another home by July.

My father and brother agreed I would move from Poughkeepsie to the Bronx with my father. I hated the idea. I had dreaded living with my hard willed father. I dreaded moving to New York City, of which I had heard some nightmarish stories. I didn't want to leave my school, as any teen wouldn't, with just one more year to complete. I resisted and voiced my objections. With few viable options for housing available, my father and brother lost patience with my resistance.

On the day I was to leave Poughkeepsie, on the way to the train with my suitcase, I acted out, overcome by emotion, triggering my father to angrily put me out of the car. My father and brother drove off, leaving me alone on the side of the road with my suitcase and nowhere to go. I looked in each direction, and didn't know where to turn. I grabbed my suitcase and began to walk to the only refuge I knew in my new country: the school.

I walked to the school and found my counselor and mentor, Miss Felter. Terrified, I called my mother in The Gambia. She complained, "This is why I didn't want you to come to America so soon. You're just too young!" The women in my life went to work, from thousands of miles away. She was able to contact a Gambian friend who had helped my brother with a place to stay previously. He was quite unwilling to lend a hand again. Not again, he declared, but my grandmother, trained in the griot tradition of diplomacy convinced our Gambian friend that I would become a blessing to him once he gets to know me. She persuaded him to help me out.

That night, I had to meet my new roommate at his workplace at midnight. I walked 1.5 miles to the hospital where he worked. I was exhausted, emotionally and physically. Finally, we arrived at the rooming house where I would live for almost a year. I was assigned a tiny room, too small to even fit a queen sized bed, more like a closet than a bedroom, to be honest. That's where I laid my head that night: a small room, alone, the moonlight invading the darkness of my new home, another stop on my immigrant journey.

While I never saw this split coming, in part because divorce was so rare in our culture and family despite tremendous personal hardships, I nevertheless embraced it with an optimistic view. It shaped me to become the person I am today. Living on my own and going to high school was an experience I will never forget. I learned the true meaning of responsibility. I learned that my life was defined by my decisions because, every action I took, if I did not carefully evaluate it, would significantly cost me in the future. I had to learn to take care of myself. I had to pay my way, alone. The idea of making a budget and balancing it became a crucial aspect of my life. The concept of juggling school and a job enabled me to develop multitasking skills. These conditions made me temporarily put my vision worries on hold.

The Walker

For most of my life, I felt guilty for my vision condition. I felt inferior in most circumstances. When I was working at A&B Supermarket, I used to walk fifteen minutes to catch the bus at 3:45 pm. every day. It didn't matter whether it was raining, snowing, windy or sunny; I walked in all these conditions.

On my way to work, I always bumped into this lady, Aisha, who is also from The Gambia, at the corner of Forbus Street and Hooker Avenue in Poughkeepsie at 3:33. The only difference was, Aisha would be driving and I would be walking. She always honked and rolled down her window to say, "Hi Alhassan, have fun at work." Among all The Gambians in Poughkeepsie, I was the only one without a car.

Since none of them were aware of the challenges I had with my vision, my friends made all sorts of assumptions as to why I didn't drive. Eventually, I was labeled "the walker," a title I definitely despised. But since I could not do anything about it, I did not have any choice but to accept it.

Social gatherings brought painful experiences for me within The Gambian community. It was during these moments that my inability to drive became a painful reminder of my vision problem. As Gambians, we love to party. While everyone else came to the parties in their nice cars, I asked for a ride, took a cab or walked to the party. During moments like those, my guilty emotions would trigger and I would feel so humiliated, my self-esteem significantly decreased. All I did during those moments was blame God. What did I do to deserve this? Why am I being punished?

For a long time, I did feel as if I was being punished. Whenever I looked back on my life, I could not figure out what I did wrong. Among all my family members, immediate and extended, I was the only one with this disease. According to doctors, Stargardt is a genetic disease that is usually transferred from a dominant gene. If this is the case, I used to ask, then why just me? I used to be so envious of my brother, Sankung, especially when I saw him driving. I would pray, cry, and be depressed about my condition a lot.

Besides guilt, I was very fearful of my future. I was always worried whether I would ever find a partner who would love me for who I was; fearful of whether I would amount to anything in this world; fearful of being worthy and fearful of going blind. Among all those fears, however, was the fear of being lonely. I was always under the impression that no one would be willing to marry me because of my condition.

The other destructive emotion that affects the quality of our life is self-doubt. This emotion creates a sense of inferiority in us. We all at some point or another have doubted ourselves whether we admit it or not. Have you ever asked yourself, *am I good enough? Am I beautiful enough? Do I have what it takes to succeed? Do I have the qualities necessary to make it in this career or industry?* These sorts of questions release an energy that does not progress our mission in life, but it instead makes us settle, or worse, give up.

Namie's Roof

What does it mean to push yourself? I truly did not understand this until a day in June of 2002. I don't remember the precise date, but I vividly remember the day. It was a Sunday evening. My home phone rang: a call from The Gambia. At that time of the evening, I knew something had to be wrong for them to call me. Typically, these sorts of phone calls mean someone in the family passed away. On this particular day, no one passed away and no one was sick, but, the voice at the other end of the phone did sound as though a serious disaster had occurred.

As soon as I picked up the phone, I heard a voice that made my heart sink. It was my mother and, as always, she used few words to make her point. However, what was different this time was the low tone and somber voice that she expressed her message through: "Today, the unimaginable happened. Your Grandmother's roof collapsed from the heavy storm and parts of the building are now crumbled."

Growing up in The Gambia, the potential of something like this happening was a constant worry. The three months of the wet season nightmare for us typically begins in Mid-June until the end of September. These were the "months of uncertainty." During these months, we would be in constant fear of losing our home. My grandmother's house was made of corrugated sheets. The structure of the house was not very sound since it was not carefully planned or built. Thus, in order to maintain the house, it desperately needed renovation, a renovation that my grandmother could neither afford, nor find the resources to support.

When I heard my mom's voice uttering those words, a chill went down my spine. What we'd feared finally came true. This was a moment of truth for me. I was put in a place in which I had to choose between rebuilding my grandmother's house or enroll in college, as I had planned.

I was faced with a critical decision whether to put my future on hold and take care of the woman who had given me so much, or to pursue my current plans of going to college and getting my degree and a job so that I could build my own house before I turned 26.

It quickly became clear to me that this was not really a choice. I am what I am today in large part due to the sacrifice of my grandmother. She fed us, put us through school and made sure we had all the necessary tools we needed to live a normal and joyful life. How could I then forgo the needs of such an exceptional individual for my own personal fulfillment?

As I thought about what to do in this case, I suddenly remembered the last advice my grandmother gave me as I was leaving The Gambia for the United States: "You can only know where you're going in life, if you never forget where you came from."

Reconciliation

I can certainly relate to the words of the great Bajan pop singer, Rihanna's hit song. All I did was work work work work work work. A house to build. A family to support. And a new life in America. A senior in high school, struggling, not sure if I would graduate on time at the end of the semester, and college on hold, I recognized that this would be a major detour on my journey.

My living situation would improve at least. After living about six months in that closet of a room, too small for a queen sized bed, my brother and his new wife, Amy, invited me to come back to live with them. My brother had met an amazing woman. After his divorce from his first wife, and all the regret which came with it, he was fortunate to meet a woman who was as devoted to family as he was. She was American, from Sullivan County. They had been together since 2001.

When Amy heard about my difficult living conditions, she insisted that I should come and live with them. This gave my brother a huge sigh of relief. After our eviction, and the episode that night when they put me on the side of the road, he felt horrible. After all, he was my older brother and had a responsibility to look after me. The emotional toll of leaving me alone was immense, especially since he hadn't the financial means to support me. Now we could reconcile our brotherhood after we both learned important life lessons. So in the last five months before graduation, I lived with my brother and we became closer.

My brother Sankung and his wife, Amy

My nieces and nephews: Left to Right: Binta, Mariama, Sankung Jr., Malang

Left to Right: my brothers Sankung, Kinda (A.K.) and me

Graduation

Two weeks after hearing about my grandmother's collapsed roof and the implications to my life here in America, I graduated from high school. Despite all the struggles -- the moving about, the late nights, the poor grades, the temptation to quit -- somehow I prevailed to reach this milestone on a long, bumpy and dark road. It really came down to the last minute, for I had just taken and passed the state English exam just three days before graduation. Had I failed, I would have had to attend another year of high school. I had already failed the exam twice. But with the support of Miss Felter, who always believed in me and encouraged me despite my setbacks, I made it. This sweet moment was one bright spot in an otherwise dark time of my life – a testament to patience and perseverance. The day had come.

The afternoon graduation was attended by my family and friends: my brother and his new wife and infant, Steward, as well as several of our Gambian friends in Poughkeepsie. The graduation ceremony was overwhelmingly emotional, from the processional march to the traditional graduation music, entering the auditorium to raucous cheers from embarrassing family and friends, the clapping and elation – it made me feel that I had done something important and memorable.

That evening, we all assembled for a party to celebrate my milestone. America! Education! Hard work! These were the immigrant ingredients of success. I called home to The Gambia and spoke to my father, mother and grandmother, who were equally elated even in the midst of their worry. As always, we prayed. I was proud of taking this step, knowing there were many more steps to take.

I knew this, in part, because of my brother, who was my quiet mentor even though we had never sat down to talk about what he expected of me, or how he would help me through the trials. In fact, he was rather hands off. But he was always there, serving as a role model, a template of how to strive in America. I could emulate him, copy his every move, and I did. He had gone to college, while he worked and raised a family.

Unlike many of my other fellow Gambians and extended family members here in America who were stuck like most Americans in low wage jobs, my brother chose academics and professional development. It seemed only natural for me to do the same, whether out of sibling rivalry or family pride, I didn't have far to look for the next step to take. I have continued to follow him and he has continued to lead me – ever so silently – to higher and higher places.

From That Piece of Sh*t to Holy Sh*t

The night of my graduation was when I started my second job as an overnight store clerk. While getting around at night was difficult, the brightness of the lights in the store made it easier to maneuver. Little did I know that this would be a turning point in my life. The lessons from the decision to give back to the woman whose wisdom made me into the person I am today completely transformed my life.

There are no accidents in life and none of us was made to live a life of inferiority. Every challenge, regardless of how gigantic or tiny, was purposefully designed to get you to your destiny. It is only a matter of choice that determines whether you use your situation as an opportunity or as an excuse.

When I took on that second job at L & P Supermarket instead of going to college, I was at a crossroad at that moment. But serving the needs of my grandmother far outweighed the desire to better my own life at that point. While working at night was something that was unthinkable, given my vision condition, deep down, there was no question that it was the right thing to do. At the end of the day, always listen to the little voice in your head and regardless of how difficult the task may be, if you feel that it is the right thing to do, then go ahead and tackle it head-on. Will you make mistakes? Of course! But, again, there are no mistakes, but lessons. By the way, mistakes are a good thing, because it is through making mistakes that you will gain experience.

Earlier I had mentioned that the decision to get a second job to help build my grandmother's house had become a life-changing experience for me. Imagine finishing an eight-hour shift lifting 50 pound bags of potatoes, onions, bananas etc., from 4p.m.-midnight, (well, 11:53 because I had to get to my second job by midnight and I had 7 minutes to walk from one place to the other), and right after finishing that shift, I had to go and do the same thing in another grocery store for another eight hours. This was physically tiring, emotionally draining, and mentally fatiguing. But do the people who hire you care about that? I think we all know the answer to that. However, you should not judge people for not caring about your condition because they hired you to complete a task; they did not hire you because they felt sorry for you. Therefore, completing the task was their top priority, and became mine.

One of my lessons came the first night at my second job. It was during our lunch break, which was technically breakfast or a really late night dinner, at 3am. As I was attempting to take a 15 minute power nap, I heard couple of my coworkers having a conversation about me.

"What do you think of the new guy?" Dave asked.

Kipp responded, "Why do they hire people like them? You know that piece of sh*t isn't going to last a week? They're a bunch of lazy bastards."

For a second, I thought of walking into the room to confront them, but I thought to myself: what good could come from that? Imagine having a confrontation with two of your coworkers on the first night on the job.

Even though I had a 100% right to confront these individuals, I knew that when you get into conflict with people, regardless of how much wrong they have done to you, it somehow tarnishes your reputation. As I was contemplating on what to do, one of the last pieces of advice my grandmother gave me when I was leaving The Gambia came back to me.

"Brusselinko, regardless of what happens, always keep your eyes on the Big Picture and always press forward." I remembered her asking me her usual question, "Do you know why the rearview mirror is smaller than the windshield?" It was during this moment I decided that the best course of action was to move on and prove to my coworkers that I was not a "piece of sh*t."

When we returned from our lunch break at the grocery store, as tired as I was, as sleepy as I was, those words, "Why do they hire people like him," kept ringing in my ears. I was not only salvaging my reputation, but the integrity of the "them," whatever that means. I adjusted my kneepad, cleared up my price gun, rearranged the aisle and then made ready for battle. From 3:30 to 4:15, I finished stocking that entire aisle, which had 38 boxes. Typically, it should have taken me at least two hours to complete that aisle. I walked up to my boss, Andrew and told him:

"What aisle do you want me to do next?"

"What do you mean?"

"I mean, what aisle do you want me to do next?"

"Well, finish the aisle you're doing first."

"It's done."

"WHAT?" His voice clearly indicated that I was either confused or did a horrible job of stocking the shelves.

"Come on, let's go check." he said. "Holy sh*t, child! This is amazing. Oh crap. I shouldn't call you 'child'. I hope you are not offended."

"No, I'm not."

"By the way, do you mind if I continue to call you 'child?' I don't know why, but I just like saying that."

"Not at all."

"Ok great."

"You can go to aisle 9. Take it easy there. It is the water and soda aisle, the boxes are much heavier."

"Ok, no problem."

Within an hour of starting the water and soda aisle, I walked up to Andrew, and said those interesting words again, "where do you want me next?"

"Oh come on, don't tell me you finished the aisle."

"Well, you can come and check."

He and I went to examine the aisle, and it was organized as it should be.

"Child, that's great. Now, you're going to join the old guy and help him finish his aisle."

Andrew was working in the pet food aisle, which is his typical aisle. On an average night, we all usually do two aisles. So I was three hours ahead of my completion schedule. As Andrew and I were stocking the shelves together, we started talking and getting to know each other. He was very shocked when he found out that I just completed an eight hour shift from A & B Supermarket.

"How in the world do you do that?"

"I don't know." While I did not fully comprehend how I was able to do that. I did know one thing for sure: I needed to keep that job so that I could successfully re-build my grandmother's house. Secondly and more importantly, I had to be the best that I could possibly be so someone, whoever the "them" is, in the future would not be prejudged due to their background and suffer the indignity because of things beyond their control.

In my long conversation that night, there was one question that was surprising to me. Andrew asked, "You are not originally from the United States, correct?"

"Yes, I am originally from The Gambia."

"I could easily tell," he said.

"How?" I asked.

"Well, you act like you're a product of your country. We had so many pieces of sh*ts who typically last two nights at most. But I've a feeling you'll last longer than that."

I just did not know what to make of his statement, and I was not fully aware of America's racial history at the time. I told him, "Well, with the grace of God, I'll last longer than two days."

As I continued to excel night after night, I was given the title "The Child" since I was the youngest crew member. Six months later, I was given a full time position, and six months after that I was promoted to the assistant manager position. Thus, the folks who called me "a piece of sh*t" one year earlier were now calling me "boss." What a difference a year makes.

Moving to the Mansion

After graduation, my brother and his new family decided to move closer to her family in Monticello. I would need to find an apartment, but, at this point I had the financial means to support myself. Two jobs. Sixteen hours a day on two shifts: one from 4 pm to midnight and one from midnight to eight in the morning. This I did for six years, which allowed me to send money home to rebuild Namie's house. As I began to look for an apartment, Steward invited me to live in his beautiful home. His parents were no longer able to visit as they had in the past, so there was a room for me. I could keep him company and also save more money. I gladly accepted his gracious offer. The sunlight was breaking through the clouds as a new day arrived in my life.

Moving into what I considered Dr. Pickett's "Mansion" was a very positive turn in my life. What an amazing influence he was in my life. I moved into a huge room in the Pickett Mansion with two large windows, bright and sunny, large enough for a queen sized bed and I felt like a king, with all the comforts of home. All I had to bring with me was my clothing.

Living with Steward meant so much to me, both financially and personally. A scholar, and a gentleman, his home, as I mentioned, was filled with books and he was filled with wisdom, compassion, intelligence and humanity. He recognized that we are all spiritual beings living a human experience, and lived his life that way. It was not unusual for him to invite children from the neighborhood for BBQs, where he would share his home, his food and his insight on life, always seeking to lift up the left behind.

He has had a lasting impact on my intellect and my understanding of American culture. The entire environment at the Pickett Mansion was cerebral and uplifting. It was there that I became a "NiPpeR," one who listens to National Public Radio, NPR, a station devoted to impartial news and information. We listened to NPR every morning, in the car and in the evening whenever we could. I learned so much listening to NPR, from foreign policy to domestic; arts, culture, history, politics and much much more. To this day, I am a loyal NPR listener and contributor, thanks to Dr. Pickett.

In addition to NPR and all the books, Steward subscribed to many magazines, including: Time, the Christian Science Monitor, and the Atlantic, all of which would spark deep discussions on a wide range of topics. That's what we did; talk, especially at dinner and when he'd take me to various restaurants at least once a week.

One of those topics was race. As a new arrival, I was not keen on the history of race relations in America, especially since my high school teachers gave such cursory attention to history. Through Dr. Pickett, my resident professor, I learned a great deal about being a black person in America, and I learned something I had never suspected: Dr. Pickett, himself, was half black. No one would know from looking at him, and he never made a point of it. I began to learn from him about the social structures and foundation of racism in America. One of our rare indulgences was watching the Wire, an HBO fictional series about the rough urban terrain of Baltimore.

I began to get a deeper understanding of race, compared to the superficial and even stereotypical beliefs I, and my fellow immigrants from

Africa, had been fed by the media. In all of our discussions, however, Dr. Pickett never expressed any anger about the plight of Blacks in America. He insisted that we could not allow ourselves to feel like victims, but that we, nonetheless, should never ignore the reality. On that, we concurred, for I have found that immigrants, even Black immigrants, seldom saw themselves as victims, rather as fortunate to come to a place with so much promise and opportunity compared to our homelands.

In addition to all the academic depth he provided, Dr. Pickett also exposed me to the finer aspects of American culture: fine dining, art and culture. In our frequent outings to restaurants, I learned the finer points of social etiquette and how to dress like a successful American.

It was not long before I would have a personal encounter with race in America. One summer day, I was riding my bike in our neighborhood in Poughkeepsie. Without warning, two police cars – one in front and one behind -- stopped me and asked for my identification. I complied and they explained that there had been a break-in the previous night and the suspect was a Black man on a mountain bike. Surely, I thought, that description described many Black men in the summer in Poughkeepsie. But, I complied, as I always do.

Not believing that I lived in the neighborhood, they insisted on accompanying me to the Pickett Mansion. And so I took them there, unlocked the door with my key, and they, finally convinced, left me alone. I was now officially a "nigger" in America. I bear no ill will to the police officers, recognizing that they were as much victims of societal ignorance as I was innocent of their fears about me. My cooperative attitude may have saved my life that day.

I owe so much to Steward Pickett for my personal development. For the four years I lived with him, he treated me like his son, and I consider him one as well.

My Friend, Bintou

The reconstruction of my grandmother's house was completed in December of 2002. I was ecstatic for the completion of this huge undertaking, so I went back home to join my family for the moving-in prayer, which is a big tradition in The Gambia. It was great to be in the company of family members who were very pleased for what had been done for my grandmother. Far more important than anything else on my trip was the ability to look my grandmother in the eyes and say, THANK YOU! Thank you for being there for us. Thank you for instilling values in us that have helped shape the course of our lives. Thank you for the invaluable pieces of advice and words of wisdom that continue to guide our lives. Looking back at that moment, I remembered the night I made the decision to postpone going to college and instead pay to rebuild this incredible lady's house. Sometimes it is hard to know whether you're making the right decision, but in those circumstances, it is imperative to remember the reasons why you should or shouldn't do something. If the *why* is clear enough, then the *how* will absolutely show up.

Three days prior to my return to the United States, I came home around 4pm, exhausted after a long day of errands. My Grandmother and my older sister, Fatou, were about to visit one of The Gambia's high-ranking officers at the Department of Immigration. They asked me to come along with them because my presence could make a difference in her being able to get a passport faster. I declined, and then they started begging me. Half an hour later, I reluctantly agreed, but I was extremely unhappy about going on the trip. On our way to the main highway, I was not part of any of their conversation because I simply did not want to be there.

While we were waiting for the bus, I turned around and saw a girl who looked like Bintou. I said to myself, no, this cannot be her. I took a glimpse at her one more time, but I was still not sure. It had been three years since I last saw her, so she has grown a lot. I secretly asked my sister "Is that Bintou?" She said "Yes." All of a sudden my mood changed. I went from being cranky to being cheerful. It is funny how we could easily change our life by simply changing our state.

My initial mindset going on that trip was, *if I am this exhausted, why am I going on this trip?* Therefore, my mood was not pleasant because of the poor state I was in. But, as soon as I confirmed that that was Bintou, all of sudden, I changed my posture. I stood up straight and began to feel energized. We all hopped on the bus and I started talking loud hoping to get Bintou's attention. At some point, my grandmother started teasing me because my entire family knew how I felt about Bintou. "I thought you were exhausted? Why are so energized now?"

All three of us started laughing. Little did I know but my loudness on the bus, trying to get Bintou's attention, was actually having the opposite effect. Bintou would later tell me that she despised me so much at that moment, because I "talked a lot."

When we got back home, I asked my little sister, Mariama, whether she had Bintou's phone number. She did not have it, so she got it from one of her friends the next day. I finally called and spoke to Bintou two days before my return to the United States. I told her how I felt about her and she just started laughing hysterically.

"How can you love someone you don't even know?" "Of course I know you and you know me too." I explained the times we stared at each other on our way back from school, and that she had been at my grandmother's house several times before to braid her hair, and that we just met on the bus the day before. The more I talked, the more she laughed.

She finally said, "You know, even though I don't know you, you seem like a nice person. Why don't we just be friends?"

While I didn't like that outcome, I accepted the offer. At the very least, we would begin to get to know each other.

~

When I arrived back in the United States, it began to dawn on me again that my prognosis was now six years away. What would happen to me when I become legally blind? Who would take care of me? Where would I be staying for the rest of my life? I needed a home of my own so at the very least, I would have a permanent place to stay without burdening anyone. Buying a house in the U.S. would be very expensive, especially if I wanted to pay it off before I turned 26. Thus, the logical approach would be to buy a house back home in The Gambia. While moving back to The Gambia would not be my first choice, especially with my physical condition, it was the most feasible thing to do financially. Therefore, I decided to buy an empty piece of land and build it the way I would want my house to be. At the very least, I would accomplish one dream in life, the idea of living in my own house.

Bintou and I became good friends in early 2003. I made it a ritual to call her every Sunday at exactly 6 pm in The Gambia and 2 pm in New York. We would have long conversations. We had so much in common, a similar philosophy of life, but particularly with our families. Her family was from a long line of political elites, a higher social class than my family, and wealthier. Her great uncle (her grandfather's brother), Sir Dawda Kairaba Jawara, served as the first president of the independent Gambia. Her father was the former Minister (Secretary of State) of Economic Planning and Industrial Development and also came from a Noble family.

Far wealthier than we, they lived in an impressive compound in our town. They even had a lawn, a rare luxury in the dirt roads of our small town. Though the family fell from power after the 1994 coup, they were still considered nobility. Additionally, our grandmothers were close friends. My grandmother, the griot, would sing praises to her family, and so the families knew each other well.

Later in 2003, her family also migrated to the United States. She hadn't even told me she had come to America for several weeks. She was focused on school and her professional aspirations. She was serious and I respected her enormously. I was drawn to her religious piety as we both came from devout Muslim families. I was impressed by her mind, discipline and her strength. She was like all the women in my life: determined, passionate, devoted, driven. There were no weak women in my life and I intended to keep it that way. And yes, the very sight of her gave me joy beyond belief.

We continued being good friends until March of 2004 when we officially started dating. Because we started out as friends, we knew a lot about each other and we trusted each other. Not only did she become my partner, but she also became my source of joy, motivation and inspiration. Her thoughtfulness and compassion towards others taught me a great lesson.

Despite being so emotionally close to her, I was always afraid to bring up my vision problem. Even though I knew deep down that she would support me with this challenge, because that's just who she was. I thought that there might be a slight chance that she would not want to spend the rest of her life taking care of a blind person. Unfortunately, I did what I thought was the best thing at the time, and did what I was a master of: hiding behind my veil of something I could not control.

The reality is, you can only pretend for so long. At the end of the day, the truth will always surface. Bintou actually found out by accident. Since her arrival in the U.S. in August of 2003, she was living in Minnesota and I was living in New York. One day, I forgot my phone at home, so I used one of my coworkers' phones at A & B Supermarket to call her and to let her know about it. She and I would talk for hours every night while I was at work, so I needed to let her know that I wouldn't be calling her that night. But she did not pick up, so I left her a message. She called back a couple of hours later but I had already left for my second job. Lou, the person whose phone I used to make the call spoke with her and told her "Alhassan just walked over to L & P Supermarket." She asked, "What happened to his car?" "What car?" Lou asked. She was now confused. "His car," she replied. "Alhassan does not have a car?" I had led her to believe that I did.

The first question Bintou asked when we spoke the next day was, "So, you don't have a car?" At that point, I was shocked and humiliated. I simply didn't know where to begin. "Well, that's a long story," I said. She replied, "And I have all the time in the world." After going back and forth, I told her I had to go and would explain to her later that night. This was one of the scariest days of my adult life. Where do I even begin this conversation and how could I make her understand why I did not tell her sooner after being together for over three years?

As soon as she called me that night, as you can imagine, she was anxious to know. Without hesitation I told her, "My vision impairment prevents me from getting a license to drive." "What vision impairment?" After few seconds of silence, she asked, "When did this happen to you?" "It did not happen to me, it is part of my life," I replied. "What do you mean?" Obviously she could not understand, given that we'd been together for so long and thought we were very open to each other. I went into the stories of my discovery of the vision problem. After hours of emotional conversation, we finally came to an understanding. We made another promise to each other--we would not hide any secret from each other ever again.

That marked a new beginning for us. We took a step closer to commitment, as a couple and not just as friends. Upon her invitation, I went to visit her in Minnesota. It was the first time we had set eyes on each other for over a year. It was wonderful.

The Wedding

As Bintou continued to support me and be by my side, I began to have hope for the future. While I was living with worry, doubts, and guilt, I was beginning to be more confident than I ever was. During those years, she was going to St. Cloud State University in Minnesota and I was building my house in The Gambia. In the middle of 2006, during her junior year, I proposed marriage to Bintou. She accepted. We decided we would get married and move in together while she was in college.

We decided! But that was simply not enough to bring this proposed union to fruition. We were African, which meant we would need to get the blessing of her father – a tall order, given the difference in our social standing. As expected, Bintou's father, the nobleman, would have no part of our plans, though her mother could care less about class. She simply wanted a good husband for her daughter, whatever his class. For a year and half, we sought his blessings. Following our traditional ways to resolve such matters of tribe and family, the elders appealed. Her grandfather, the patriarch of the family, would ultimately make the final appeal. I visited him and he liked me, simple as that, and he said he would have no trouble accepting me into his family. In this day and age, when social classes are converging in a new world order, he felt his granddaughter would be well served by a man of my background, even though my family was not noble, nor wealthy. He would convince Bintou's father and we got his approval.

The building of my house in The Gambia took longer than usual, but I finally completed it in December of 2007. I went back home for the moving in prayer. Bintou also came home to be with me to celebrate this wonderful occasion. On December 30th, 2007, on a Sunday, 4000 miles away, Bintou's father gave his permission for us to marry. We were delighted. We were home, all of the family present, so we decided we would get married that Friday, just five days later!

What a week that would be! We had five days to plan a traditional African wedding, considered a cultural event of the highest order, representing the creation of a new family and the continuation of the original family, like a new branch on a tree. It is a huge social phenomenon, with explicit requirements and expectations; more so, since this wedding would unite two families – a family of nobility and a family of griots. Since we were already pretty well connected, the task would be somewhat less arduous.

Though we had no need for formal written invitations, I would need to visit all the members of my future wife's family to introduce myself. We would need to plan the festivities, pass the word along, and sew the fine African cloth into the fancy garments the bride and groom would wear. As the groom, my family would need to buy all the food, including a cow, for the feast of many.

Then there was the matter of the dowry, an ancient custom involving the transfer of wealth from the husband's family to the family of the bride. I would present 5000 dalasi (Gambian currency, about $200, a great deal of money back home), and another cow. Still common in parts of West Africa, the dowry symbolizes the weaving together of two families, interlocking them into eternity. We are a part of that tradition, which has somehow survived into the 21st century.

My house in Gambia, completed in December, 2007

The preparation was underway. Mostly the work of the women who would cook, and sew, and weave, and arrange, and choreograph one of the village's most important occasions. And not just any wedding; a griot's wedding, and the bride from a noble family. But also, this was a Muslim wedding. The entire village's men gathered at the mosque for prayers and the official blessing ceremony. This was strictly a religious rite, not even requiring the presence of the bride and groom, for this was a matter of utmost importance, requiring the attention of the elders to preside. No, this was not like going down to city hall to get a marriage certificate.

At around 2:30pm that Friday afternoon, my cousin informed me that I was officially married. "Welcome to the club!" I phoned my wife, who had been at the Salon doing what brides do at salons. We shared a deep emotional moment, just a moment, for now we were getting ready for the party of the century. I wouldn't see her until that night when the entire town would gather for an outdoor feast. Night time! The fear crept in, once again. I never socialize at night! My sight, or my lack of it, was a well-kept secret and I was not ready to reveal my greatest weakness to the entire town that night. I decided I would not attend my own wedding party.

I went to my home compound to enjoy the excitement of my family and friends who were all assembled for a day and night of celebration. When I called my wife and told her of my plan not to attend, she would have no part of it. "We'll find a way to make it work," she assured me as she always does, loving me and accepting me unconditionally, my partner and my friend.

I got dressed and prepared to come out that night.

My brother drove me there, perhaps a short 20 minute ride. Needless to say, I was very anxious. When I arrived at the compound, I noticed many more lights than usual had been strung up and I could see well. My anxiety was beginning to dissipate. Had she arranged this, I wondered?

It was a huge outdoor feast for the over 500 guests who had arrived that evening. When I entered the reception area, the people were assembled in a large round circle. Bintou rushed over to me, gave me an enormous hug and kissed me as the women shrieked and screamed with excitement at the rare public display of affection, even from a bride on her wedding day! She and I wore matching wedding outfits, cut from the same cloth; white linen, embroidered with elegant stitching. Me in a kaftan, her in her gown. She was absolutely fabulous! I was now married to the love of my life. We were each other's first! The woman I respected before I loved. The woman who embodied the essence of what I wanted from a woman: wisdom, strength, compassion, devotion, resourcefulness.... like all the women in my life.

My grandmother was never surprised that I would marry a woman of Bintou's stature. She knew all along. She would tell me that those were the seeds I had planted. Seeds of giving, of caring, of devotion. She knew there was someone for me as I had been there for others. Her voice rang in my ears that glorious night.

The party was a blast. We had traditional griot musicians singing praises to all the family members and sharing the stories of our families' roots: our lineage, our background, where we came from. Each song was dedicated to a specific person who would dance in the center of the circle as praises were sang to them, while receiving gifts of cash from both my family and Bintou's.

As the evening wore on, the older family members left as the younger members shifted from traditional music to contemporary African beats. We danced all night to a live DJ. Bintou and I hardly had anything to eat. She never left my side. We were always together, happy and celebrating our new life.

After spending a week on our honeymoon in The Gambia, we returned to the U.S. because my wife had two semesters left to complete her Bachelor's Degree in Minnesota. I went back to New York.

OUR GAMBIA WEDDING

~

Imagine crawling down on the floor from one aisle of the store to another. From one corner of an aisle to the other, arranging products on the shelves and putting the misplaced products back to their rightful place all night long. While you're doing this, you happen to be hanging out with someone who has been doing the same "sh*t" for the past 27 years. This was our typical night on Wednesdays at L & P Supermarket. Andrew and I were usually the only people in the store on this night because there were no deliveries on Wednesdays.

However, the night of Wednesday, January 16th, 2008, was not just another ordinary day at work, but a turning point in the trajectory of my life. Andrew and I had been talking all night long about life and the decisions he had made in the past, and only if he could have turned back the clock. But as we all know all too well, we cannot change the past events of our life.

"What has been the biggest accomplishment of your life?" I asked him.

"I have a beautiful and loving wife. I am not worried about money, and I don't owe anyone anything."

By this standard, most people would be very happy with their life. How would your life be if you were 100% debt-free? How would your life be if you had a loving and caring partner who unconditionally loved you? This would be a dream life for most people. In his "21 Elements of Success," Jackson H. Brown explains that 95% of a person's happiness or misery depends on their marriage/relationship. Given the high divorce rate in the U.S., if you're lucky enough, like Andrew, to be in a healthy and loving relationship, that is something definitely worth celebrating. Despite all of these great things going for him, Andrew was unhappy with his life.

"What would you consider as your biggest mistake in life?" I asked.

He unequivocally replied "Doing this sh*t."

While I was not completely surprised by his answer given our prior conversations, I was reminded on this particular night about my life's current path. I thought of being in my fifties and looking back on my life as a failure despite being in a great relationship and not worried about money either. I imagined crawling down the aisles with an 18 or 20 year old, twenty years from now and telling him that the only thing that sucks about my life is doing this "sh*t;" I also thought of leaving my family home on Thanksgiving night, after eating until I could not walk anymore, and then dreading going to work that night. Or, instead of being home on New Year's Eve watching the ball drop with my wife cuddled under my arms and kids sitting next to us, I am at work. None of these scenarios sounded attractive to me or made me happy about my future. I then began to put things into perspective and it was that night I stopped making fun of Andrew. In the past, I always made fun of him when he complained about how the job sucked.

This was the night I realized that Andrew's problem was larger than his complaints. His problem was lack of meaning for the job. In other words, he was not fulfilled by what he was doing. Instead of seeing himself as someone who adds value to society by leading a group of people whose livelihoods and whose family's wellbeing comes from him providing them with a job, rather than seeing his position as providing goods and services that help members of the community, Andrew has narrowed his job to simply stocking shelves. As I mentioned earlier, it is never the events of our lives that give us pain. It is, however, the response we choose to associate with those events. Our response automatically creates how we feel, which ultimately determines what we end up doing.

By most people's perception, Andrew would be living a very happy life. Part of the challenge in this situation was that Andrew could not find meaning in his "success." Success means different things to different people, and everyone needs to be able to define what success means to them. While there are different methods of defining success, and different measures of it, I find Earl Nightingale's, one of the earliest thinkers of the personal development industry, to be a useful definition. Success, according to Nightingale, is the "progressive realization of a worthy ideal." In other words, if a person is working towards a predetermined goal and s/he is able to achieve that goal, that person would be considered a success.

For Andrew, and all the people that I worked with at L & P Supermarket, they were not fulfilled with their job or life in general because the job they ended up doing was never intended to be a lifelong career but it ended up being so because they felt stuck after a while. After years of hoping that their lives would change, after unintentionally having kids and starting to build families, after looking in the future and seeing no other way out beside *what they could see*, my coworkers did what 84% of the workers in the United States do according to Pew Research. They hate their jobs but continue doing it anyway because, as one of my coworkers beautifully put it, "You gotta to do what you gotta do to pay the bills."

When I got back from lunch that Wednesday night, it finally dawned on me; I didn't want to live this kind of lifestyle. I took the overnight position to rebuild my grandmother's house, now that that's done, and as much as I was comfortable in my current position, I knew my life had a bigger purpose even though I was not sure what that purpose was.

PART IV

He who has been bitten by a snake becomes scared by the sight of a rope. –Hausa Proverb

College

As soon as I got home that morning, I ate breakfast, got on my bike and went to Dutchess Community College.

"How can I help you?" the receptionist at the registrar's office asked.

"I am here to enroll in college."

"Did you apply?"

"Yes, six years ago."

"Oh, okay, what took you so long, boy?"

"Well, that's a long story, but let's just consider that history."

"What program do you want to enroll in?"

"I don't know."

"Do you know when the semester started?"

"No, I don't know that."

"Boy, did you just wake up from a dream and say to yourself am going to college?" She smiled.

"I don't know, but something like that."

"Ok, when can you take the placement test?"

"Can I do it now?"

"Sure."

After working all night, sitting for a placement test was daunting. But when I thought about what this would mean for my future, the pain of complaining about my job for the rest of my life outweighed the pain of lack of sleep for one day.

After three hours of taking the placement test, I came back to see the lady at the front desk with my scores. I did very well in all the subjects except one, math, of course. Mathematics had been the most challenging experience for me throughout my secondary school education.

~

Thinking back, my high school Algebra teacher once said in class that I would drop out of college if I ever enrolled. While he did not clearly mention my name, it was obvious who he was referring to. He asked me to solve a problem, in front of the class, and I was sitting at the back of the class pretending to be a normal sighted student while I should have been sitting in the front. Instead of telling him I could not read what was on the board, I told him what was convenient. That I didn't know the answer.

"Well, I think we know those who will drop out of college if they ever go."

Ten years later, I would remind this teacher of this sentence when I was training to become a teacher and went back to my former high school to observe classes as a student-teacher.

During the lunch break, when all the teachers gathered, I joined them to have the teacher's lounge experience. All of a sudden, here he comes -- my former history teacher asked the algebra teacher, "Hey do you remember Alhassan?" He looked at me and did not seem to ever remember me being in his class. I became adamant because I wanted him to remember what he told me ten years earlier. "You should vividly remember me. I used to sit in the back of the room and I was always too quiet. I always had trouble solving the homework problems on the board."

"Which class were you in?"

"Algebra I."

"Oh, that's why. I don't usually care about that class."

"Oh really, why is that?"

"Well, honestly, no offense, but that's where they usually put all the dummies."

I replied sarcastically, "and that's where the people, who would drop out of college if they ever even make it there, would be placed?"

"Well, I won't go that far," he replied.

"You know, I was in that Algebra I class, but I graduated with honors from The University of Vermont."

"Well, congratulations. It's great to see a successful student from this school."

At that point, all I wanted to do was to tell him that there would be a lot more successful stories from that school if people like him would stop instilling limiting beliefs and instead help those kids to have bigger dreams and aspirations about their future.

~

After reviewing my scores, the lady in the registrar's office asked which classes I would like to register for. "I don't know." "Well, boy, is there anything you do know? Because, so far, all your answers to my questions have been I don't know." She was actually right, I had no idea what I was doing at Dutchess, I didn't know what classes I should take, I didn't know what degree to pursue, or for that matter, what career I should embark on. I had no idea what this experience would be like.

Despite all the things I didn't know, there were two things that were particularly clear to me that morning: First, I was very scared about attending college for so many reasons. But my biggest fears were how I would be able to see the board and, after not being in school for six years and working two full time jobs, whether I could pass my classes. But the most important issue that I knew for sure was, I DIDN'T WANT TO LIVE MY LIFE WITH REGRETS AND BE COMPLACENT LIKE MY COWORKERS AT L & P SUPERMARKET.

Given that I didn't have answers to the receptionist's questions about class selection; I told her I would like to register for an English class and a Math class, which was coming back to what I did know. I knew that regardless of what field I went into, these two classes would definitely be applicable. She made a schedule for me and said, "You'll begin classes on Monday."

"Good luck Mr. Susso, I am confident you'll do well."

My first thought was that finally, she was not referring to me as "boy." But more importantly, I needed to hear those words, "I am confident you'll do well," because I wasn't sure whether I would do well. But the idea of spending the rest of my life frustrated about my job was enough reason to get me started on this new path. I got back on my bicycle and started heading home feeling euphoric. It felt like I was taking control of the direction of my life.

I put in my resignation letter the next day at L&P, but they asked me to not quit. I could work part time, and they would still pay me my full-time hourly rate. I agreed. Now, I would be juggling two jobs with college classes. While thinking about it was painful, at least I felt like I was moving forward.

~

I took Sunday night off in anticipation of my first day of class. It felt like attending school for the first time. Remember those feelings back in kindergarten or first grade? By the second or third grade, most kids are already tired of school or are typically not as excited as they used to be. Although I was excited about attending college, at the same time, I was very scared of the "what ifs."

My first class was my Math class and it started at 8:30. I came in at 7:45 to check out everything. Luckily, the room was open. I walked around trying to figure out the setting. Of course, the number one thing being how close did I need to sit to be able to see the board? Around 8:15am, this short older looking African-American woman walked in, and it was clear that she was the professor.

"Hi, my name is Alhassan, I am a new student."

"I am Ms. Johnson, welcome."

One by one, the students started rolling in. At exactly 8:30, Ms. Johnson started the class. As she started writing on the board, I was beginning to get nervous, but fortunately, I could recognize what she was writing. It was a small class, about twelve students in the room. I was able to participate and it seemed like my ideas were making sense.

When that class was over I headed for my next class which started at 10 am. When I walked in the room, the class was nearly full and the professor was already there. All I could think was, I hope there is a seat in the front. I was lucky enough to find one seat in the front row. This class felt slightly different from my earlier class. The students were more focused and the classroom environment felt more structured. I would later learn that the professor has a reputation of being a "no nonsense teacher." I walked up to her and introduced myself.

"That name sounds interesting, where are you originally from if you don't mind me asking?"

"Oh, not at all. I am from The Gambia, a small country located on the west coast of Africa."

"Interesting, I have some friends from Nigeria."

"Yeah? Nigeria is about a two hour flight from The Gambia."

This is a typical response from most people that I come across. They either have a friend from Nigeria, Liberia, Ghana or Sierra Leone. Not surprising, I hardly meet anyone who can even identify The Gambia on the map, never mind having friends from there.

Nonetheless, the professor seemed friendly and welcoming.

"I am Ms. Wiley, and these are the books you'll need." The day's lesson was about writing patterns for different genres. This was a bit confusing since I was one week behind schedule, but it appeared to be interesting and intellectually stimulating. By the end of the day, I felt very happy with my decision, but now it was time to go back to work. Since I had not slept in the morning, this meant that I would be awake for 30 hours straight. This would be my new normal. But I did understand this principle: temporarily sacrifice with massive pain is far more crucial than slow consistent everlasting pain.

Day after day, week after week, month after month, I juggled two jobs with college responsibilities. While it seemed like things were going well, I still had doubts about my performance.

~

Throughout my life, I've doubted myself in almost everything I did. While in high school, I never thought I would make it, because I could not speak as eloquently as my classmates. What I did not know at the time was that just because someone could eloquently express themselves did not necessarily mean they were smarter than me. It was not until college that I would discover this.

One day, I walked into Ms. Wiley's office and asked if I could speak with her. My facial expression clearly indicated that something was wrong.

"What's wrong, Alhassan?"

"Well, I don't think this is the appropriate class for me."

"What do you mean?"

"These kids are so smart. They speak so well and they always finish the exam so fast." (I was typically the last person to leave the room.)

"And, what's your point?" Ms. Wiley asked.

"Well, I am not smart enough to compete with these kids."

Ms. Wiley burst into laughter, which was surprising to me, because she was usually a reserved individual. After her inability to stop laughing for a while, she finally said.

"Well, I am not sure what to tell you." After a few seconds, she continued, "Let me show you this. I think this will help."

She went into her school account and showed me the entire class grades without compromising the privacy of the other students. She asked me to make note of the highest grade in the class, and then she asked me to log into my account and check my grades. As it turned out, my grade matched the highest grade in the class. So, while I was feeling inferior in the classroom, I was actually at the top of my class.

It was during this moment I got my first lesson about overcoming self-doubt. Ms. Wiley asked, "Do you feel that you're doing your best?" I replied, "No." "Then that's what you should worry about. Furthermore," she continued, "our only competitor in this world is our self. You should measure your progress based on producing your authentic self rather than devoting your energy on what others are doing or not doing." While I have doubted myself in subsequent events, I never doubted myself in Ms. Wiley's class.

~

My negative self-talk and self-doubts about whether I was on the right path took another turn for the better in the middle of the semester. I attended a mandatory seminar for minority students. Dutchess is a great community college with an impeccable reputation for academic excellence; however, it also has a significant minority dropout rate. In 2007, the year prior to my enrollment, it had an 80% minority dropout rate. Thus, a seminar was held for minority students to create options and provide information and resources for reducing this problem. At the end of the seminar, as I was leaving the room, Ms. Wiley gave me a handwritten note. When I left the room and opened the note, it simply stated:

"Alhassan, after 40 years of being an educator, you're the reason I still do this."

While this was a flattering note, I took it as a general compliment, and continued to do my best.

Honestly, I did not fully comprehend the meaning of the note but I took it as a compliment anyway. It was not until the last day of the semester, after everyone left, when I went to thank Ms. Wiley for treating me with respect and dignity in her class, that I understood what that note represented. This was when she elaborated on the note. "As a young man with lots of ambition, focus and a clear sense of direction, I am honored to be able to contribute to expanding your worldview a little bit more. The kind of work ethic you have, if you continue on that path, you'll do great things in this world. You can do whatever you set your mind to, young fellow. Keep pushing forward." After an emotional hug, I told her "Thank you! This means a lot to me."

What Ms. Wiley did not realize that morning was that she became a transformational teacher for me. She believed in me when I constantly doubted myself. She gave me hope when I at times felt hopeless. She took me out from the dark into the light. She helped me cross the bridge from not knowing about my potential to knowing that it was possible to live my dreams.

That summer, I took five classes. I went from trying out college to becoming a full blown student. I was ready to move forward with my college education because I knew it was possible. For the first time in my life, I was beginning to find that precious aspect of life that creates lasting happiness: I was beginning to find meaning for my life.

Death Strikes Hard

In the summer of 2008, as I was very excited about my future, shifting into high gear, gaining confidence, settling down financially and accomplishing important goals along the journey, I encountered yet another mountain to climb, or more accurately, I was on the precipice of a deep emotional chasm.

My little sister, Binta, was diagnosed with Hepatitis B. After the diagnosis, we learned that Gambian hospitals didn't have the necessary resources to treat her illness. She would need to go abroad for treatment. I began to coordinate this process with my family to find doctors and hospitals in the U.S. for Binta's treatment.

A daunting and frustrating task, but eventually we were able to gather all the necessary paperwork and finances to get the process started. To get her medical visa, we had to put up $25,000 in cash as proof we had the financial capacity to take care of her adequately. While together, my father, brother and I would be able to take care of her, no one had that kind of ready cash sitting around.

Then another angel appeared to me, in the form of my boss Andrew, with whom I had developed a close relationship while working for him the past six years. He had quickly abandoned his preconceived notions about Black people and we grew to respect each other on more than an employer-employee basis. Based on a strong, reliable work relationship, in which we worked closely together and talked a lot during the evenings, we became friends. We were close. I knew his secrets and he knew mine.

When I came to Andrew and told him how much money I needed in order to get Binta here for emergency medical treatment, he didn't bat an eye and told me he would help and brought me the $25,000 in cold, hard cash the very next evening. What a friend!!! Suddenly, I grew optimistic, but soon that optimism evaporated into steamy frustration.

~

When Binta went for her visa interview in September, the visa Consular denied her visa without any explanation. We did everything we could to challenge the decision administratively and legally, hope dimming by the day.

On Friday night, November 14th, at about 7 pm, while I was working at job number one, I was eating a slice of pizza on my lunch break when I received a call. It was from The Gambia, where it was around midnight, so I knew something was wrong. It was my father, who was back home.

"Hello." I said, as I anticipated the worse. He came straight to the point. "Your sister, Binta, has passed away." I don't quite remember what happened after that. I just fell over crying uncontrollably. Twenty minutes later, the entire crew of the grocery store surrounded me, trying to comfort me.

Eventually, I pulled myself together and called Steward, but he didn't pick up. I took a cab home and called the family compound in The Gambia. I spoke with my mother and grandmother for hours. I called my brother and started to make arrangements to fly back to The Gambia as soon as possible. In our culture, burials must take place within 24 hours of death.

Left to right: My late sister, Binta and my big sister, Fatou

Namie's Heart

Binta, our youngest sister, lived a sad life, in part because of her order of birth and gender. I was five years older than Binta, and another boy would follow her seven years later.

Until Binta was born, I had been the baby of the family and my grandma's sole focus. So, as with many children, I was jealous of my little sister for years because she took a great deal of my grandmother's attention formerly reserved for me.

When she was born, she basically became Namie's baby. Their relationship was incredibly special. Of all her grandchildren, Binta was Namie's heart. Namie knew this child drew a short straw and she did all she could to shield her from the reality that she was not the family's top priority. The boys, of course, were favored by nature of our patriarchal culture, girls always taking second place. In my family structure however, my older sister, Fatou, the queen of our house was everyone's boss. This left Binta with little wiggle room for getting anyone's attention at the house beside Namie. Alone and confused, Binta was always quiet and reserved since no one would listen to her opinions. Namie, who loved her the most, would often beg for prayers for Binta's health to improve, or, she promised, that if Binta died, she would soon follow, an ominous thought to us all.

Sadly, Binta was forced into a marriage she didn't want at the age of 17 to one of our cousins 18 years her senior, a decision my entire family lives to regret. She didn't want to get married and resisted fervently, causing chaos in the family. Ultimately, she relented, for sadly, she had no choice in the matter. Not long after, she got sick, and now she was dead. We were not just sad, but also felt guilty for not having been more involved in her life. We had failed our sister and now it was too late to make amends.

~

I had been on the phone with my family in The Gambia for hours, making arrangements for myself and my brother to return home. About 3AM, after I had just closed my eyes for a short slumber, I received another call from The Gambia, from my father. Not fearing any worse news.

"Your grandmother just died!"

"Are you joking?" I asked incredulously. He was not.

I felt like my heart had stopped. I was overwhelmed with intense physical grief.

My grandmother died as she promised, not long after Binta, of a heart attack. We knew her heart was broken.

My brother and I flew back home that morning to join our family, soaking silently in a stew of sadness and regret, with a generous dollop of guilt mixed in. Binta had died. Our sweet 19 year old sister was gone. Namie was dead. Our beloved grandmother was gone. My North Star had burned out and I felt rudderless and empty. I felt horribly guilty about how I had resented Binta as a child, and how things had turned out for her. My brother's feelings, though shrouded in silence, could not have been much different from mine.

Departing New York's JFK Airport, we arrived in Senegal at 7 the next morning. There were no flights to The Gambia until later that evening, so we took a cab for five hours and arrived about 2 o'clock in the afternoon. We had missed Namie's funeral ceremony, which was held during that morning's prayers, as per custom. We stopped at my father's house, which was not far from my grandmother's.

As for my mother, she was stunned into speechless silence with the sudden catastrophe which had just struck home. The shock overtook her, as she got swept up into her responsibilities for preparing her mother and her only daughter for immediate burial. This was not unlike many cultures, where women serve the role of family caretaker, especially when death intrudes.

On our walk to her compound, we saw cars lined up for blocks leading to her home. The whole town was mourning the passing of my grandmother, a testament to the woman she was and how much she impacted the lives of so many. She had been a leader in our community, known by all for her compassion, wisdom and judgment. Many outside our family relied on her for advice and counsel on the most important problems in their lives.

Along the way, we met a woman, standing forlornly.

"Your grandmother was supposed to come to our house today to help us solve our marital problem. What will we do now?" she wondered. Namie's influence was felt far and wide. Yes, she was a nationally renowned griot, but she was much more than that. She was one of the town's most revered elders. Few people had her level of diplomatic skills. She was a wise negotiator, as I had learned many times, in many difficult situations which seemed hopeless. No one could say 'no' to her. Since birth certificates were not issued when my grandmother was born, no one knew her exact age. By best estimates, she was about 86 years old.

Even until today, nearly a decade later, people can remember where they were when she died. Her presence is continually missed and she is forever remembered because she was always concerned about others. She always gave more than was expected and there was never a problem too big for her to solve.

We went to the graveyard that evening. My grandmother and my sister were buried right next to one another, emblematic of their lives together. Somehow, we knew it had to be this way. The funeral brought the family both a sense of closeness and closure.

My brother returned to America after a week because he was teaching. I was able to stay for a month. Even though I had been in college, with less than three weeks before final exams, my professors were incredibly supportive and graded me based on the work I had done up until that point in the semester. I earned all A's.

~

I began to think about my college journey. I enrolled in college because I wanted to make a better life for myself and my family, but I had no idea what I wanted to study. Now, I had a mission in this world. That mission was to ensure that I was going to do something in the future that would ensure that another family would not go through a similar situation. Well, one might ask, what would be a noble field to pursue this journey? Since we're talking about the injustices in the world, why not become an immigration lawyer. This way, I would really be able to help prevent another immigrant family from going through a similar experience as my family.

With a vision of where I was heading in life and passion to make a difference in the world, I excelled in all my classes. I even got an A in Math. I made it onto the President's List, which was the highest honor from Dutchess for academic excellence.

My wife, still living in Minnesota with her father and siblings, was completing her education. In December of 2008, she graduated from St. Cloud State University with a degree in Electrical Engineering, an amazing accomplishment for a girl from our small town. Her excellent academic record landed her a job with one of the most prestigious computer companies in the world, IBM. She was offered a job in Burlington, Vermont, and he accepted the position so I transferred to the University of Vermont after completing my first year at Dutchess Community College. We had already been married a year, but we had never lived under the same roof together. That would change now.

Bintou and her brother, Dawda, flew in from Minnesota, while my brother and I packed a U-haul and headed for Vermont. This was an end to another long journey. It was my departure from Steward Pickett's Mansion, an emotional end to a wonderful four years together. When we arrived in Vermont, we were welcomed with a blanket of gorgeous, pure white snow, both cold to the touch and warm to the senses. It snowed for 19 days, as if as an extended greeting. That year, we lived in three different apartments, until we found the right size to meet our meager budget. Dawda, who had lived with us for six months, returned to Minnesota, I was in school and my wife was impressing all of her colleagues and supervisors at IBM.

Vermont is an exhilarating place. Vermonters are some of the nicest people you'll ever find in the U.S. While not culturally diverse, Vermonters have a great sense of respect and dignity for humankind and the environment. They're welcoming and tolerant of other cultures, so the two and a half years we lived in Vermont were filled with joy and harmonious interaction with others. Vermont still holds a special place in our hearts.

~

At the University of Vermont, I continued to excel academically and had great relationships with my professors. Since I was planning on going to law school when I completed my undergraduate program, I majored in Political Science. The University of Vermont did not offer a Pre-Law Program.

All was well during my first two semesters at UVM. I was part of the debate team, The Mock Trial Club, and helped rejuvenate the Muslim Student Association with a fellow from Iran named Ali. I was quite active in the school community, but my academic performance was my top priority.

Since law school was my next stop, most of the classes I took dealt with constitutional law, argumentative writing classes, and philosophy. During my third semester, I took an "Introduction to Logic" class to help boost my reasoning skills. What an experience!

The logic class was held in the Carpenter Auditorium in the Givens building, a huge auditorium with wooden seats and a high glass ceiling. I am not quite sure how many students the auditorium holds, but by the time of my registration, there were 178 students in the class.

All excited and looking forward to more intellectual conversations about various topics regarding the use of logic; coming to class that first day was quite exciting. The class took place Tuesdays and Thursdays at 1pm. On the first day, as I finished my Political Theory class and walked towards the Givens building, I was quite pleased with how everything was progressing for me at UVM. But that excitement would quickly turn into a nightmare.

When I entered the Carpenter Auditorium, I quickly paused at the door—"holysh*t--this is a huge classroom. How am I going to make it here?" For a moment, my heart rose and fear crept in. As I began to go down the rows one step at a time, I kept looking straight at the projector screen. With every step, I was more and more scared because the lights were already dimmed. When I looked up, I could not see what was being projected on the screen. I carefully made it down all the way to the first row but there were no seats available. I tried the second row, but no luck there either. On the left corner of the third row, a girl said: "Hey, there is a seat here." When I took my seat, I was slightly relieved. At least I could stop bumping into people. But that moment of relief quickly turned into more irritation as I could not see anything that was being projected.

It is safe to say that I did not learn anything that day since my entire focus was: how am I going to survive in this class? At the end of the class when the lights were more lit, I walked up to the professor. "Hi, I am Professor Weiner," he said. "Is this how this class is going to be?" I asked. "What do you mean?" he replied. "Well, are the lights going to be dim all the time and are you going to be writing on the board or constantly using the projector?" "Well, the lights will only be dimmed when I need to project on the board." "Is there a problem?" I paused for a second and said, "no." "Thank you for your time, Professor Weiner." As I walked away, I was convinced that I should drop that class given that the classroom setting was not conducive for my situation, but the syllabus looked quite interesting.

Tuesdays and Thursdays were torture. Right after my Political Theory class, I would rush to Carpenter Auditorium to get the front row before the lights were dimmed. Day after day, week after week, month after month, I sat in that wooden hardback chair staring at the board not seeing what was written on it. I would listen carefully to Professor Weiner's explanations, but since the problems we discussed were number problems, my technique of carefully listening to the teacher's explanation without seeing what's written on the board was not effective in this class.

The first exam came; I got a D, the second exam a C. Every moment of that class brought agony, frustration, and sadness. At the end of every class period I would say to myself, "Go and tell him you need support for your inability to read from the board." Another voice would say, "that's a bad idea." "What could he possibly do for you?" or "Your classmates would know that something is wrong with you." I was never worried about Professor Weiner because he was a nice person. Whenever I would visit his office for help with the course, he was quite willing to lend a hand. This was why he was always puzzled with my exam results, given the effort I'd put in the class.

By the end of the semester, I received a grade of D+. While not necessarily surprising, this crushed my spirit, but more importantly, it significantly decreased my GPA. The reduction in my GPA would make it harder, if not impossible, to get into the law schools I was aiming for.

I went to talk to Professor Weiner about it but he was not interested in any excuses. Who could fault him for that because the one thing that students are masters of is making excuses for their low or failing grades. My only other choice of improving this grade was to retake the class. But the class was going to be held in the same room, the same professor, the same material and yes, the same challenges for me. Therefore, something certainly needed to change in order for me to increase my grade the following semester.

With the support and advice of my wife, I decided on that day that, since I did not ask for this vision problem and it was not my fault, then I was just going to be honest about it and people were entitled to their opinions. I walked into the student services center and talked to a counselor about my situation. When the paperwork was completed, they immediately gave me services for my summer classes such as, extended time on exams, taking the exam in a bright quiet room, and providing seats for me in front of the classroom so I could see the board better.

When I took the Logic class again the following semester, Professor Weiner made a copy of the lesson for me every single class. While he was explaining from the projector, I was following along on the papers he gave me. He would constantly check-in with me to ensure that I was keeping up with the pace. At the end of the semester, I received an A.

For things to change, I had to take action. I could not be doing the same things and expect a different result. You might be wondering why I didn't say something in the very beginning. For me, this was a big step; a far cry from my upbringing where a disability becomes a stigma, as if it was your fault. You become 'lesser than.'

Citizen Susso

Becoming a citizen of the United States of America is a prize to people all over the globe. America has always been a beacon of hope to millions from all countries, cultures and continents. No matter what your politics or place in society – doctor or deliveryman – America is the place to make your dreams come true. Ever since arriving in America, I dreamed of becoming an American. I immediately applied for my green card when I arrived in 2000 and received it four years later after already having a lifetime of experiences in America. After coming to America already, I was becoming American.

As soon as I could apply for my citizenship – about five years after receiving my green card – Bintou and I went to the immigration office to file for our official applications for U.S. citizenship. I remember the day we went, specifically my interaction with the immigration clerk. As part of the interview, I explained that I was a student of history and political science at University of Vermont. He chuckled as he asked me the mandatory questions about the basics of American civics. After one or two questions (How many U.S Senators are there?), it became obvious that this part of the interview was a waste of time. He shared what he loved about his job. He loved helping people achieve one of the most important accomplishments possible: becoming an American. He told the story of a 94 year old woman whose last remaining dream in life was to be an American and how she had died just five minutes after he swore her in as a citizen. I understood exactly how she must have felt, for I had the same dream.

Two months after we applied, Bintou was sworn in as a citizen. From then on till I received my papers, she joshed me. "Now, who's an American?" she would tease. But in September, I too dressed up and went to the courthouse to become an American citizen. It was a thrilling moment for me. It was particularly fulfilling to recite the "Star Spangle Banner." I chose to maintain dual citizenship. While I love my new home and will probably live my entire life here, I knew I would forever be linked to The Gambia. I had come a long way since arriving here ten years earlier with not even a clue. But here I was, married, working, enrolled in college, on my way to a career in law, and I hadn't even begun to make a difference in my new homeland.

Eye Test

By now, I had managed quite well with my vision impairment. I had been in the country for almost ten years. Despite all my fears, my visual acuity had not deteriorated any further. The sentence of blindness by 26 had not come to fruition, even though the idea never escaped my deep consciousness. I went every year for monitoring, and every year, the verdict was postponed.

If I was baffled, the doctors certainly were as well. My doctor told me that the disease was unpredictable. It had not progressed, but the diagnosis seemed to be changing. The original damage to the center of my eyes' retinas, thought to be consistent with Stargardt, now looked to be more like the disease Retinitis Pigmentosa or RP. People with RP experience a gradual decline in their vision because photoreceptor cells (at the center and the margins of the eye) die. For some unknown reason, my condition was frozen in place. My eyesight was stable. The doctor quickly warned me that I should not get my hopes up too high, but to remain confident. I was reminded of what my grandmother often said, "The doctors can say all they wish, but only God can do what he pleases." In other words, man proposes, while God disposes. I moved forward with that faith.

~

I moved quickly through college for several reasons.

First, I felt like I was getting old, so I needed to finish in order to start my career. Second, my sister's death gave me a sense of urgency and mission in this world. Lastly, I was fast approaching 26 years old and the thoughts of what could happen to my vision were constantly on my mind. Each of these made it all the more urgent to complete my bachelor's degree quickly. My wife and I spent countless hours in the library doing research and writing and editing my papers. I certainly would not have been able to achieve as much as I had in college if it wasn't for her emotional as well as intellectual support.

I scheduled myself to graduate May of 2011 rather than waiting for an extra year, which was my original graduation date. This came at a price of course. On average, I took 18-20 credits a semester, while at the same time, preparing for the Law School Admission Test (LSAT).

I was scheduled to take the LSAT on December 12th, 2010. Most students typically take the LSAT in the spring of their junior year or the fall of their senior year. During those times, I was focused on completing my courses to stay on track for my May 2011 graduation. At the same time, in order for me to enroll in law school the fall of 2011, I needed to take the December LSAT. But the LSAT in December happened to be the week of final exams at UVM. As anyone who has been to college knows, this was a hectic week on campus for both students and professors alike. It certainly was even more complicated for me.

I was trying to complete my final exams, research papers and study for the LSAT at the same time. The Thursday prior to my LSAT exam, I stayed up all night to complete a paper for my National Security Policy class. I thought that, since I would have the entire day of Friday to rest, I would be fine. Terrible idea.

I showed up for the test on that Saturday morning. I had never been as tired as I was that Saturday morning since leaving L & P Supermarket. I was physically, mentally and emotionally drained. I was placed in the room with students who needed extra support due to their disabilities. There were about eight of us in the room.

As soon as I sat down, I started to fall asleep. Not merely dozing off, but a real deep sleep. The test proctor came over and asked whether I was okay. I was fine. "I am just sleepy," I told her. "Well, you need to be alert in order to perform well." "Yeah I know." I ended up using the restroom 8 different times, washing my face and trying to take 5 minute power naps. Most of these actions were not allowed during the LSAT, but the proctor was concerned with my well-being.

But, regardless of what I tried to do, nothing seemed to work. It was some of the longest five hours of my life. I typically don't like giving up, because I am a believer that quitters never win and do not amount to much in life, so I tend to work extra hard when the task seems unachievable. But on this day unfortunately, I eventually gave up after five hours of simply trying to stay awake.

~

Prior to taking the LSAT, I put together my law school application, gathered all of my letters of recommendation, references and all other necessary documents. I was just waiting for was my LSAT test scores to turn in the application. I chose to apply to New York University (NYU) Law School because it had a great immigration law program and an outstanding clinical program as well. But after my LSAT debacle, I knew that the possibility of acquiring the score necessary for NYU Law School was slim. It ended up just as I predicted.

After receiving my LSAT score, I went to meet with my advisor, Professor Lisa Holmes. She evaluated everything and her recommendation was to retake the LSAT again in February because my score would not qualify for acceptance to NYU Law School. I could try to apply to other less prestigious law schools and I would probably be accepted into one of them since my entire application looked solid with the exception of my LSAT score.

If I retook the LSAT in February, I would not be able to start law school until January of 2012. Time was of the essence for me. I was not willing to do wait. I put my head down and was clearly disappointed. Professor Holmes tried to comfort me by saying, "Hey, Alhassan, this is clearly not the end of the world." One of the things I admire about Professor Holmes is her straight-to-the-point advice. She does not sugarcoat anything; she gives you the honest, pragmatic and sincere advice.

After being clearly distraught, professor Holmes said, "Actually, I don't think I ever asked you this question – why do you want to go to law school?"

All of a sudden my mood changed because that was something I was always passionate to talk about. I told her about my sister's story and that I wanted to ensure that another family would not go through such a painful experience.

"I want to help immigrant kids," I replied.

After thinking about it for a while, Professor Holmes said, "That's great, but don't you think at that point the battle is lost?"

"What do you mean?"

"Well, by the time you defend them in court, they are either about to get deported or going to jail. Why not do something that will actually empower them so they never have to see the courtroom?"

After a pause, that question hit me, "why not empower them so they would never see the courtroom?" I was really excited about this idea. So we started brainstorming ideas of how that would look like and what career could achieve this goal. I came to the conclusion that, as Nelson Mandela said, "education is the most powerful weapon that you can use to transform the world." I therefore decided that I was going to become an educator. How? I didn't know. Again, never worry about the how. If the WHY is strong enough, the how will always fall in place.

I came home that night and told my wife, "guess what?" She just stared at me as usual waiting for something crazy to come out of my mouth. And surely, she wasn't disappointed. "What do you think about me becoming a teacher?" She bursted into uncontrollable laughter. "Who gave you that crazy idea?" I replied, "Professor Holmes." "Well, I don't think that's really a good idea." "Why?" I asked her. "Well, first, you're very impatient, and kids can sometimes be annoying." After few hours of talking about it and looking at the pros and cons, she said, "if you really want to pursue this path, I'll support you and I believe you can achieve anything you put your mind to."

Well, on that night, my real concern was not my lack of patience, but something much bigger. How would I be able to clearly write on the board for my students? How would I be able to read their hand writing? How would I be able to watch a movie with them with the lights turned off? As I began to dwell on these thoughts, my wife actually said, "you can do this." She never wanted me to use my disability to limit myself on what I could achieve in this world.

After a couple of days of research and conversation with people, most teacher training program application deadlines had passed. My sister-in-law, Amy, happened to find one program whose deadline was three days away, the Bard College Master of Arts in Teaching. With the help of my professors, we put together the entire application, plus all of the supporting documents and mailed it via overnight express.

After evaluating my application, I was accepted into the program. They also accepted me into the fellowship program which was designed for a select group of students committed to teaching in New York City. I later discovered that Bard's NYC location was at a high school called International Community High School (ICHS). ICHS is a high school comprised of only immigrant students. The qualification for attending the school is that you have to be in the country less than four years. ICHS is part of a network of high schools for immigrant students. Wow, is that a coincidence or what? It was not a coincidence. When life feels like it's falling apart – it's actually not, God is rearranging your path a little bit so that it can all come together in the end.

Leaving Vermont

I am forever amazed at how quickly situations can turn around, from seemingly bleak one moment to blissful the next. So too, for me. One moment, I discovered my dreams of a career in law were dashed; the next, I would choose a career I may have been groomed for since I was a little boy back home in Africa.

Now that I had found a job and a graduate school program all wrapped up in a neat package, we didn't have much time to get re-settled back in New York. We had only a month to move. My classes would start just three days after I graduated from the University of Vermont on a Sunday. That Friday, I was expected to attend the opening reception at Bard.

My wife was able to transfer from IBM in Vermont to their Fishkill, NY location. Conveniently, we would live in Poughkeepsie, and I could commute to work in New York City, while my wife had a shorter commute to Fishkill. Things were falling nicely into place. Luckily, we found a two bedroom apartment on the Southside of Poughkeepsie, right next to Steward's house, which we stumbled on while going out to dinner with Steward while house hunting. It could not have been better, living so close to our dear friend. Now that we were citizens, we could send for our immediate family members. Soon, my mother would be coming to America.

My wife excelled in her career. She was an exceptionally gifted team member and presenter, considerably quite articulate, particularly for a woman in a male-dominated field. She was already considered a leader with great potential. When she arrived in Fishkill, she picked up where she had left off in Vermont, her reputation having preceded her. Soon, she would be invited to present at the weekly Vice President's Conference, in recognition of her leadership and excellence. She eventually was promoted to train all new engineers, a critical job for the company.

By now, we had been married for over three years and we had been hearing a mounting chorus of calls for a baby from day one. In our culture, wives are expected to have children right away or suspicions will quickly arise that she might not be able to bear children. Such was the pressure on my wife. Her mother was beginning to worry and the family was waiting not so patiently. My wife, the new American, didn't worry too much about these requests for a rapid pregnancy. She was committed to starting her career well and we wanted to put ourselves in a better place financially before taking this important next step. We started getting ready to start our family.

I remember when we found out Bintou was pregnant. It was November of 2012. We had been in Springfield, Massachusetts at a business convention where we received an award. After we returned that night, Bintou awoke me at about 1 AM and told me, "You're going to be a father!" I was speechless. All we could say was, "WOW!!!!" over and over again. We prayed, thanking God for this precious gift, and asked for his guidance every step along the way.

At that moment, my sense of what life meant changed immediately. What would happen, I wondered? What about all of the peace and quiet which we had grown accustomed to? I thought about how I felt when my brother brought his four children over and all the chaos that ensued. We knew we would have to change our mindset about life right away! I would still have lots of growing up to do. I was also a bit worried about my role as a father for I hadn't had much of a role model in my father who had left for America when I was only two years old. I had grown up with all strong women and would need to learn how to be a father. This was not much of a concern for most Gambian men who saw their role as a parent to be limited to baby maker and provider. Parenting, in our culture, was for women as far as I knew and saw.

In addition to these questions, I secretly feared that my child might suffer the same genetic fate as I and inherit my vision problems. We talked about it and spoke to the doctors who said that the genetic inheritance patterns can be recessive or dominant. There was really no way to predict without some extensive genetic testing. We reconciled these fears by concluding that either way, we would leave these matters in God's hands, since we had no control anyway.

Mother Arrives

2012 turned out to be a momentous year for our family. I had built a house in The Gambia. We were getting our house in New York in order. Now we were in a position to bring our family together, one of the most persistent values of our culture. It was time to bring my mother to America as she was the matriarch of the family, now that Namie had passed. When we got her Visa, I went home to get my mother to bring her to her new home.

We arrived on Sunday, March 18th, 2012 to America as I had several years earlier, at JFK Airport. I decided to travel with my mother because she spoke no English and had never before traveled so far. She wore a grand outfit, called "Garanbubo," a traditional African garment associated with elderly women. She looked like a true African Queen and carried herself as such. Like me, and all new immigrants, she was astonished by the sights and sounds of America. When she came to the "moving steps," she looked puzzled. "I aint getting on that," she insisted. "I know exactly how you feel, Mother," I concurred. After a meal of Dunkin Donuts on our way from the airport, she was now safely tucked in America.

Meanwhile, I was well on my way to becoming a teacher.

First Year Teacher

At the end of the 2014-15 school year, two Peace Corps fellows, Jen and Kelly, interviewed me about my teaching experience and asked if I had any advice for new teachers. Jen and Kelly were student teaching with two of my colleagues and had observed my class on different occasions. I have one philosophy about classroom visits: you're welcome to visit anytime as long as you don't disrupt my classroom or the flow of my instruction.

I walked into my classroom one day and there was Kelly sitting at my desk. "Can I observe your class first period?" As always, my response was the same, "yes." I proceeded with my morning preparation and welcomed my students at the door as always. One of the great things about the school, and my class in particular, was that there were always visitors, so my students were accustomed to having people observe them.

The lesson that day was *How to create a budget*. I did not get a chance to talk to Kelly after the lesson because I had another class right after, but she must have been pleased with what she saw. By lunchtime, Jen came and asked if she could also observe my class. "Kelly said I have to see your class. She was quite impressed." I was thrilled to hear that. I did not do any extra preparation because I was being observed. I responded to Jen, "Come in anytime." One week later, Jen walked into my classroom 15 minutes prior to the beginning of the lesson and asked to observe me first period. "Sure." I gave her a run-down of the lesson which was *Understanding Credit Worthiness*. At the end of the lesson, Jen said to me,

"This was the liveliest first period I've ever seen. Thank you so much." I was again quite happy with the feedback.

Given that neither of their visits to my classes were planned, their interview with me was not planned either. I walked in two days before the end of the school year, and right after I signed in, I heard, "Hey Alhassan." As I turned around, "Today is our last day here. Can we interview you for just five minutes?" "Sure. When did you want to do this?" "Can we stop by in 15 to 20 minutes?" After a pause, I said, "Sure."

Forty-Five minutes into the interview, we were still going on. Unfortunately, I had to stop because my students were about to come in. "Can we please come in tomorrow to continue?" "Sure." The next day, we finished the interview after two and half hours. Their final request was, "Would it be possible for you to come in and speak to our graduate class?" Unfortunately, I was unable to grant their request because I was scheduled to be out of the country during that time.

By now you must be wondering, "Wow, Alhassan must either be the greatest teacher ever or he must be really full of it." Neither would be an accurate description. What captivated Jen and Kelly were the struggles I went through my first year and how I was able to overcome them.

~

During my graduate program, I was trained by wonderful instructors who had countless hours of experience as classroom teachers and as teacher trainers. They taught us curriculum planning, unit planning, lesson planning, classroom management, student engagement techniques,

techniques to deal with administrators, etc. By the end of the program, I felt that I was equipped and ready to be a great teacher. I was fortunate enough to be the first in my graduating class to get a job. By the end of my first student teaching position, the principal at that school decided she wanted me to teach at the school. By February, I was assured that I had a job beginning in the fall, so I had a very good and relaxed summer.

When I woke up on the morning of September 4th, 2012, my official first day as a teacher, I was extremely excited but, at the same time, nervous. Even though I had concerns that first day, one thing was clear; I knew why I got into teaching. The school I would teach at, International Community High School (ICHS), had 400 students comprised of 75% Latinos, 15% Africans, and 10% Middle Easterners. My goal of empowering immigrant kids was coming to fruition.

As my students started making their way into the classroom, they gave me the strangest looks. Looks that asked, "Who is he?" "What's he doing here?" "Are you serious?" Or, "may God be with us." They were not surprising looks based on this situation. I was the first African teacher in the school, but on top of that, I was an American History teacher. I could understand their surprise when they saw me. As the second bell rang indicating the start of class, I was saying to myself, "what did I learn from my graduate program for this kind of situation?" I could not remember anything. At this point, my heart started racing and my legs shaking, but, as the only adult in the room, I had to get myself together to have control of the room.

"GOOD MORNING, Class B"

In very low voices they go: "Good morning." Over three-quarters of the class remained silent and those who responded only did so out of respect.

"Where is Ms. Catherine?" asked one of the students. Ms. Catherine was their history teacher the previous year.

"Ms. Catherine now teaches 11th grade. I replaced her."

"Why?" half of the class responded in shock. At this point, I felt like I was beginning to lose control of the conversation, so I said, "We're going to play a game. It's called *Getting to know you*." While they were not enthusiastic about the game, at least they participated. When the bell rang, we all thought to ourselves, "Thank God that's over." The next two periods happened to be my preparation periods, so the next time I would have class was after lunch. Yes, I would have time to recover from that disaster.

When my classes resumed in the afternoon, the entire school knew about me already. "Hey Mr. You from Africa?" I can assure you, there was nothing on my forehead or on my shirt that said anything about Africa. Even as adults, it does take some adjustments to adapt to a new situation. Change is a hard thing, especially in this case. Moving on from being taught by a nice, soft-spoken blonde woman to a strict, deep-voiced African man with an accent would not happen overnight.

As the year progressed, my challenges got bigger. To make matters worse, the principal's office was right next to my classroom. When students walked out or were kicked out, they would typically return with the principal or her assistant. Sometimes, I had to explain myself. Other times, she and I would just have an eye contact of understanding. All these, unfortunately, took away from valuable instruction time.

I had some difficult and hard-to-forget days that first year. On one occasion, one of my students walked in late and, as usual, any student who came after the bell rang would need a pass before entering the room. When asked for her late pass. "I DON'T HAVE ONE." "Can you please go and get one?" "You're so annoying. This is why no one likes you in this school." All of a sudden, most of the class erupted in laughter and began echoing similar sentiments. I was demoralized but needed to keep myself together in order to continue teaching. That was the first time I questioned my decision to become a teacher. However, I always remembered the genuine reason why I got into teaching. I knew something had to change, but didn't exactly know what. But I continued to hope for that miraculous change.

The second really difficult day of my first year was on a Thursday, fifth period, right after lunch. When the class started, one of the students decided to move her table around to face the opposite direction. She was provoking me because she knew that I would strongly react to that. I definitely did not disappoint her. We went back and forth for about 15 minutes as I tried to get her to turn the table back to the way it was. I ended up getting so angry that all I could think was that I wished I could grab this child out of her chair and throw her out the window. Luckily I didn't do that, but I did stop the class to call her mother. Fortunately, I did not get hold of her because I would have shared a few choices of words for raising such a disobedient child.

While these happened once in a while, they were nothing compared to my last period class (Class A). This class was comprised of all the low-skilled students and "troublemakers." There was one student, who actually happened to be from Burkina Faso (Burkina Faso is located in West Africa), who probably gave me more grief than any other student that entire year. Almost every single day, as soon as class began, when I would turn to write on the board, he would throw a book at someone to provoke them. And surely, the person would angrily attack him.

This basically meant that the class would erupt into chaos. It became so prevalent that I stopped writing on the board in order to keep an eye on him. For almost a year, this was how I would end my day. One day, as he provoked yet another student, I became so angry that I grabbed his arm and looked him in the eyes and said, "YOU ARE AN EMBARRASSMENT TO AFRICANS." He looked at me and smiled, as if it were a compliment.

Despite all of these challenges, I still continued to do what I thought was my best: creating interesting lessons and staying after school for tutoring, even though only two Bengali students came to my after school tutoring class. When the year ended, I volunteered to teach summer school because none of my colleagues were willing to do it. Again, I always remembered my WHY, but unfortunately, volunteering to teach summer school was way too ambitious because my wife and I were expecting our first child that summer.

~

I arrived to school early on Thursday, three days after summer school started, to set up everything and was ready to dive into the lesson. At the beginning of first period, which was 9am, no one had shown. By 9:05, I was beginning to worry. At 9:08, two students walked in. They looked extremely disappointed to see me. "Where is everybody?" I asked. "We don't know." After a few seconds of silence, one of the students said, "Hey, Mister, let me tell you the truth. There were 22 students in this class the first day, but when they found out you were the one teaching the course, they all dropped out." Not knowing how to respond, I said, "What are you two doing here then?" Without hesitation, "Oh we need to pass this class to graduate this summer." "Well, let's proceed so you guys can pass this test and graduate."

Although I had many difficult moments during my first year of teaching, this particular day was, by far, the most painful and the lowest point in my teaching career. Obviously, I was extremely hurt. All I wanted was to help these students and empower them to have a better future. I was also hurt because I had left my wife and new baby and traveled two hours to go to work, even though I could tell she was not thrilled about me working that summer. I was simply torn apart.

~

As those experiences unfolded during my interview with Jen and Kelly, they asked, "So, how did you go from that to this amazing teacher?" (I would not necessarily categorize myself as "amazing" because the word is so loosely used that it doesn't have the authentic representation of the speaker's intent). At that point in my career, I knew I had to change even though I was not sure how. But I did know one thing for sure: I needed to turn the situation around before the next school year began.

To complicate things even further, the soft-spoken and nice teacher, whom my students missed so much and were raving about having her again in the coming year, suddenly left the school. I was promoted to replace her. Now, I really didn't have a choice but to change. When the students walked in and saw me in that classroom, they would freak out so much given our previous year experience.

As I was heading home on the first day of summer school, I started crying and saying to myself, "I could have been in law school by now, then at least my clients would appreciate me because they would desperately need my help". But more importantly, I could have been with my family, and having a great time with my wife and baby. Not knowing what to do, I went onto YouTube, and the first video that came up was Oprah's 2013 graduation speech at Harvard. The thing that stood out to me was when she said that when the Harvard president called her the year before to ask her to give this commencement speech, she was at her lowest moment. But when she accepted the invitation, she promised herself that by the time of the speech, she would turn the OWN network around, and she did. At that moment, I also declared, "I will not quit. In fact, when I leave ICHS, I will be remembered as the greatest teacher who ever walked the hallways of that school."

Since I knew that when my students saw me on the first day of school as their 11th grade teacher they would freak out, I made a big poster that stated:

"Last year was the past,"

"Next year is not guaranteed"

"Therefore, we're going to make the best of this year."

Boy, did we make the best of that year! I welcomed them on the first day with the Bruno Mars song, "The Way You Are." They liked that song so much that we started every class with it. This small shift towards their cultural norms began to turn things around.

A big question I asked myself the summer after my first year as a teacher was, "why do people do what they do?" If you ask good questions, the right answers will show up.

I started to shift my thinking from what the curriculum dictated to reflecting on what the students needed or would need in the future. One of my biggest challenges in college was the experience of a feeling of inferiority because I was always worried about whether people understood what I was saying. This is quite typical of immigrant students because of the language barrier or accent challenges. To help my students develop confidence and public speaking skills, I developed a program called "Friday Seminar," which was not part of the original curriculum, but was something the students would absolutely need in the future.

During the seminar, everyone was required to speak. By the end of the year, each student's public speaking skills increased significantly. From that point on, my main focus was determining what the students needed.

Other things they needed for college and in life were communication and leadership skills. Therefore, I dedicated two days a month to these subjects. In order to be a great leader, one needs to develop a compelling vision for their future, so every February from that second year on, we did a Goal Workshop and Dream Board Sharing. Finally, we ended the year with Financial Literacy and a unit I called Life Mastery which looked at physical, emotional and effective decision making, and creating healthy and lasting relationships.

Since I had declared on that train that I would be remembered as the greatest teacher that ever walked the hallways of ICHS, I knew that I could not be conventional and expect to achieve this goal.

After my horrible first year as a teacher, I needed to recreate my image to succeed in the field of education. While I did not understand why the students were disrespectful towards me, looking back, I know I needed to go through it in order to become the person I am today. I understand this concept; pain is only a tragedy if we do nothing about it. Our painful experiences can be transformed into teaching tools to take us further in life. So, based on my struggles as a first year teacher, I used that experience to change my identity to a teacher that empowered both my students and me.

Based on my close relationships with my students over the years, they would frequently ask whether I would be attending prom. I always said no and if they asked why, I always gave them a lame excuse. Last year, I decided to attend prom for the first time. This took courage because I was not sure how to handle getting around in the dark since the venue was on a rooftop and I didn't know what to expect. I arrived at the site at 6pm even though I was not expected to be there until 7pm. I took the extra time to observe the different areas of the venue before it got dark. At the very least, I would be able to get around once I was comfortable with the location. As the students began to arrive, I told them I would be leaving around 8:30pm, because that was the time of sunset.

At 8:30, the students would not let me leave, and I knew those who weren't there yet would be upset if I left before they arrived. Some of the students who were running late called me to get that point across. I had formed great relationships with those students and had convinced most of them to attend. Around 9pm, a group of students formed a circle and they called me to dance and let me know that there was a huge surprise waiting for me. A surprise? Who or what could it be? Another student, an award or what? It was none of those, but was better than anything I could have ever imagined. I was stunned to see my wife surrounded by my students and everyone yelling SURPRISE. This was one of the most memorable moments of my life. Since my students knew that I've never been to prom, they secretly invited my wife so I could re-live what I'd missed in high school. The attention of the entire prom became my wife and I and I could not have felt more blessed to have such people in my life.

The point of this story is not the fun that I had attending prom with my wife, but that facing my fear allowed me to place this moment among my collection of pleasant memories and I can finally explain to my daughter what to expect at prom—well, maybe not the surprise visit by her mother. Our choices shape the quality of our lives, so let's make choices that allow us to live a compelling life.

First House of Our Own

After my mother arrived, with Bintou pregnant, we decided to bring our family together. In addition to my mother, we would bring Bintou's mom and sister from Gambia to live with us. We would need a much larger house. We started looking.

During Christmas-time 2012, I talked to my dear friend and neighbor, Steward, about our new aspirations, and as usual, he stepped right in to help. He put me in touch with his long-time realtor, Sue. After seeing many houses, and on the verge of giving up hope, Sue showed us a house in the town of Poughkeepsie, about 15 minutes from Steward's mansion. It was a gorgeous home. When we walked in, Bintou fell in love right away. It had a huge front lawn and backyard. It had a large screened-in patio in the back and behind the house was the Wappinger Creek. The view was stunning. I could imagine our family sitting out there talking loudly, as our people do, and not having to worry about disturbing our neighbors. It also had a two car garage.

Inside, there were four bedrooms on the second floor, including a large master bedroom for us. On the first floor, there was a living room, dining room and kitchen. The basement could be used as an additional apartment or office. Hardwood floors. It was perfect for us.

May of 2013 was most momentous: May 20th, my birthday. We moved into the new house on May 22nd. Bintou's mother and sister arrived in the U.S. from The Gambia to live with us, and I graduated from graduate school on the same day, May 25th. Thirteen years after coming to America, we were experiencing a culmination of all our hard work and effort -- all the detours, discomfort and distance. We had finally come home, our home, and our family would help us make this house a home. We celebrated with prayers, and praise, and together marked a whole new chapter in our lives. More good fortune was still to come.

Amina

The baby was due to arrive in late July. The pregnancy had been going well for Bintou. She continued to work. I would finish my first year of teaching and had decided to teach Summer School since my mother and Bintou's mom would be there for her when the baby came home from the hospital. I hadn't thought at all about my responsibilities as a father of a newborn baby, my first.

It was a Sunday evening, July 14th, the day before the first day of summer school. It was a quiet evening, so I went over to my brother's house —about 2 miles away. We were waiting to break our daily fast as we were celebrating the holy month of Ramadan. My mother was preparing the meal when Bintou called.

"I think my water broke."

This was a surprise because the baby wasn't due for another week. I calmly went home and took Bintou to the hospital, not telling anyone else. I didn't want to alarm everyone and set off a wave of prayers beseeching God to protect the mother and child, as is our custom. We were so accustomed to difficult deliveries in our native country.

When we arrived at the hospital, after an examination, the doctor said, "Well, you're not going home anytime soon because this baby is ready to be welcomed into the world."

What an interesting experience at the moment! My daughter was knocking on the door that would open our lives to parenthood. Until then, I thought about parenting like most Gambian men who have very little to do with children, much less, infants and delivery. Gambian fathers do not go to hospitals with their expectant wives. There was no purpose. Childbirth was the sole domain of women. Grandmothers and mothers go. This was simply natural, or so I thought until that very moment. The first time a father sees his child is when the child comes home from the hospital.

It was different for us. We were together as a family and even though our mothers were here, we felt this child was our responsibility. Perhaps I was becoming more American every day. The baby was coming, but not quite yet, so I went home. I called my principal and we agreed that I would return to work the following Thursday.

When I told Bintou's mother that her daughter was in the hospital getting ready to deliver her grandchild, she was unhappy that we hadn't told her immediately. This was her daughter, after all. I demurred to keep the peace, and explained that the baby wouldn't be coming for a few more hours. As it was sunset by then, we would have enough time to break our fast and return to the hospital. We all ate, packed up all sorts of packages bundled with love and anticipation, and went to the hospital. Even my father-in-law went along. We were all becoming more American.

We were all there that night, six of us, casting about with eager longing. It was quite moving, the two families bonding together -- everyone talking to one another, loudly and rambunctiously, as Africans do when Africans are together; thinking about the future, our future, the baby who would physically embody our collective future. After hours of waiting, the doctors sent us home at around 1 AM. They all packed up and went home, like a tribe of nomads.

Since one person would get to stay overnight, we experienced a bit of a tense moment, albeit brief. Naturally, Bintou's mother wanted to stay overnight with her daughter. This was our culture, our habit and the natural order of things as long as we had all known. Though I had until that day concurred with this worldview, I was suddenly trapped in the moment. I could not imagine not witnessing the birth of our first child. Bintou had also wanted me to stay because we had taken child-birthing classes together and she felt I was better prepared. America is where we were. Africa is where we had been. We were forced to balance those equally strong forces. I gently insisted and her mother left with the rest of our clan. They would return first thing in the morning.

That night, as her labor was progressing, Bintou instructed me on the precise moments to shoot photos and videos upon the arrival of the baby. We went over our birthing class roles and checklists. The night progressed.

By 6 in the morning, the baby started her descent to planet Earth. Doctors said the baby would be here in an hour or two. I called the family, and they rushed over. I still hadn't called my mother. I didn't want to alarm her and get her agitated. I would pay for that decision, soon. Fifteen people arrived at the hospital that morning to greet our new family member.

On that Monday July 15, 2013 at 11:27am, my wife and I welcomed Amina Susso into this world. Of course, I forgot all my photojournalism tasks and didn't take one picture at the right time. I was simply too exhilarated to think about a camera. My daughter was here. Amina. We named her after my grandmother, Namie, whom we had lost a few years earlier. I thought of Namie, and I knew how proud of us she would be. She, of course, would have been there in the birthing room, if she were alive.

I guess they call moments of intense and sudden enlightenment an epiphany. This experience for me was just that: a wave of deeper insight and consciousness flooded over, as if I had entered a new emotional dimension. This was my child. I was her father. She belonged to me and my wife, the love of my life. I saw everything with new eyes.

Even though they had always meant a lot me, my students suddenly meant more to me than they had before. Now, I felt like I had a special obligation to the children I taught, for I wanted as much for them as I wanted for my very own daughter. I recognized how important each of them was, as a special human in their own right. It was an overwhelming realization.

This was when I began to think less about curriculum and more about the student: where they were, what support they had, who would guide them, what if no one cared? Teaching, at that moment, became a calling for me, not just a career. Amina had made me a real teacher.

I gazed into her eyes as I held and cuddled her to me. I could see myself in her. Namie in her. My mother in her. Binta in her. She was ours and we were hers. I fell in love with her. Looking back, I can't imagine how some men could ever miss such a life-altering experience.

I called my mom to give her the joyous news, and as you can imagine, she had some choice words for me for not calling her sooner so she could witness her granddaughter's birth. After several hours, my huge clan departed for home. The younger nieces and nephews didn't want to leave their new cousin. The youngest one was most upset because she was no longer the baby of the family.

We, the three of us, stayed in the hospital for three days. I stayed the entire time. Bintou and I took turns at night. We were joint parents, partners in the process, together. I would soon have to start teaching summer school. Now that I had met my daughter, I regretted agreeing to teach. I had thought I would have nothing to do with a new baby. How wrong I was.

Although I thought I knew the beauty and blessings of being a parent, I could not have imagined the emotional feelings and gratitude that comes with holding your own child for the first time. At that moment, nothing became more important in life than being a parent. As I kept staring at my precious little daughter twiddling her fingers, I was constantly smiling. I began to realize that the most important things in life are what we sometimes take for granted. For the next three days, I could not leave my daughter's crib side.

The more I looked at Amina, the more surreal it felt. I remembered the nurse telling us "your daughter is very attentive. As the other babies were crying in the nursery; she was listening quietly to their cries. You should play more classical music for her when you get home." As a parent, anything good that you hear about your child is always a great feeling.

Amina's birth gave me a new perspective on life and how to deal with people. Her birth grounded me into reflecting a lot on life's most precious moments. But, more importantly, her birth allowed me to realize our common bond of humanity. We're all born the same way. We all come into this world with nothing and we'll also leave everything behind when it is our time to go. We left the hospital on Wednesday and came home. Fixing the place up to make it comfortable for Amina was a thrilling experience. Surrounded by friends and family, it was a moment that will live with me forever.

After all of these experiences, going back to school the next day was probably one of the worst days because I wouldn't have been in that position if I had made the right decision. While I considered this decision a mistake at the time, it turned out to be a turning point in my teaching career.

Amina's birth became the light in this long arduous journey as a small boy from that small town in The Gambia to a high school teacher in America's largest school district. Her birth became my guide for understanding that success is not measured in material possession, but the fulfillment that comes with being at peace with people that are placed in your life.

Regardless of how my day has been, coming home to an African home in America with Amina's footsteps running down the stairs screaming DADDY DADDY DADDY makes the sun shine brighter in my life and the moonlight more lit in our household as we look onto passing the baton to a new generation of American Griots.

My wife Bintou and I with one week old Amina on her traditional naming ceremony

Amina and I during Eid-Al-Adha in October, 2014

Amina in February, 2016

Amina and her cousins in The Gambia, 2016. Left to Right: Isatou, Amina, Sarjo

Amina and her grandma (Bintou's mom)

Amina and her cousin, Aisha in The Gambia, 2016

PART V

If you change the way you look at things, the things you look at change

–Wayne Dyer

Full Circle

A s we close this brief chapter of my personal story, I wanted to reflect on my life at this juncture in my journey. Here I am (now 32), exactly 16 years after I arrived in this new country, when I was but 16 years old myself. In just 16 years, I have battled and overcome incredible odds: a black boy, immigrant, half blind, a world away from the dirt road village in Africa's smallest country.

It therefore occurred to me that I have lived exactly half of my life in America, and half in Africa. Am I as a result of this symmetry, half American and half African? Am I less African than I was, or more American? Or am I both more American and more African? From my vantage point, I cannot tell, so I leave it to you to make that distinction.

Much has happened in the sixteen years since I stepped off the Air Afrique flight on that fateful Sunday, September 3rd, 2000. For one, Air Afrique is no longer an airline. An African-American was elected president of the United States, twice. My wife and I are now American citizens, parents, homeowners, and part of the American professional class. I survived the loss of my grandmother and my younger sister, and most of my Gambian family members are here in America, with us.

In the past sixteen years, much has changed in my small town in The Gambia. Where there used to be still water on the streets during the rainy season, now there are paved roads. There are street lights that make movement easier at night. The Old Jeshwang Primary school has been rebuilt and the infrastructure is more modern. The grueling Common Entrance State test is no more. Students are experiencing better chances of gaining education.

That compound in the small town of my birth has been relocated across thousands of miles and generations of traditions, to upstate New York. We are together, sharing meals and stories, watching over the children and looking into the future, while honoring the past. And, while all is not perfect in the new world, we accept our place in it and make meaning through our living. Our homes are still there: my father's, mine, and my grandmother's. The family continues to thrive in the motherland, with our help and our prayers.

Sixteen years ago, I left the sanctuary of my grandmother's love and protection. On her lap, I sat, because I could not wander off and play like most boys my age. On her lap, I learned more than I realized I was learning. She taught me more than I could conceive as a baby and a boy. I am still unraveling the endless spool of wisdom she downloaded onto my tiny brain, time released.

But the lessons have guided me like a shiny star against the night sky. With you, I set out to share these handful of precious lessons (simple, yet sacred), which propelled me along my way, like the wind billowing a sail. Without these gems, I could never have reached the heights I have achieved, however humble they are in reality.

So without pretense of great wisdom, or many years of experience, I would like to share a few of the insights I have absorbed in this short life I have lived thus far from the cultures around me, the places I've lived, and the people who embraced me.

Relationships and Associations

While human relationships may seem the most obvious resource in life, it certainly bears repeating, because repetition is the best teaching tool known to man. We already know that from our infancy, our personality and worldview are shaped in great part by the people in our lives. Our ability to relate to one another, to work with one another, to learn from one another, and cooperate with one another is central to our social and emotional success.

Since coming to America, my ability to survive and thrive, to a great degree, depended on the development of meaningful friendships with people I had never known before, far away from my small town in The Gambia. My ability to ignore spikes and insults, to work hard in spite of them, to be earnest, honest and generous, were keys to opening the space to form these vital and often mutually beneficial relationships.

Going beyond stating the obvious, phrased so eloquently already by John Donne, that "no man is an island," I would like to expand the admonition about relationships with one about associations, and the power of both when well managed.

One of the easiest ways to measure where you are in life at any given moment in time is to look around you. Often by examining the company you keep, you can tell an enormous amount about who you are. I have heard, though I cannot confirm it personally, that if you're with nine losers, you're the tenth. We take on the mannerisms of the people around us. We speak the way they speak. We eat what they eat. They make the same money, according to research. Have the same diseases; live in the same kinds of houses; accumulate the same amount of wealth or debt; wear the same clothing. We, as they say, run in their circles, an apt image given the restrictions of associating with people who run around mindlessly in circles.

So it stands to reason that if we want to change our circumstances, one of the first things we can do is to associate with those with whom we have common aspirations. In other words, go with those who are going where you want to go. With that mindset, it stands to reason that if you want a life filled with success and positive energy, you need to start hanging around people with success and positive energy. This is one of the simplest principles of success to follow.

I really came to understand this vital principle when, four years ago, my wife introduced me to Market America, one of America's fastest growing Internet Marketing companies. Immediately, I was surrounded by more than a network, but a family of people with a common goal of simply helping one another and finding others to help.

It was here that I began to experience the amazing power of association, outside my family, tribe and community. Here was an organization that had chosen to come together for a common cause. I will never forget hearing the personal story of the CEO, JR Ridinger, and how moved I was by his authenticity and genuine passion to help others. Everyone that I met was interested in my personal journey and story. In fact, it was these new friends who first encouraged me to write this book, and for that I am forever indebted.

Our weekly meetings in our Poughkeepsie group have become some of the most transformative moments for both my wife and I. These folks are genuinely interested in people. Their positive energy, inspiring team work, and clear vision for the future have set us on a much clearer path. I am a better teacher today in large part due to the skills I've developed from being in the company of such wonderful people. For example, it is through their seminars that I learned the development of the right mindset and attitude for success, as well as communication and leadership skills. I have used these skills to transform my students' lives. Every one of my students graduate with their dream board and action plan for how to attain those goals and I learned that from my team members in Market America. The application of these techniques in my teaching practice, not only increased my effectiveness as a teacher, but my students are forever transformed. For that and many more positive changes in my life, I am forever grateful.

The Importance of Powerful Women

My grandmother was my constant teacher, parent, and coach until the day I left Africa and every day since. She showed me how to soar in heavy winds, my head firm against the draft, eyes ahead and wings strong.

She was always with me. The most important lesson I learned was the power of powerful women.

When we think of African women, particularly Muslim women, we often imagine subservience and passivity. This perception is not reserved for African women, of course, as the stereotype crosses cultures, fostering a perception that women are weaker physically and intellectually than men, and that furthermore, this is the natural state of being.

Men born in male-dominated societies, particularly African, are often raised with these notions of male superiority and dominance. They eschew "womanly" characteristics like empathy, compassion and love, in place of aggression, force and brute strength. What I have learned throughout my life is the exact opposite. I have found that the women who raised me were incredibly strong, remarkably resilient and unstoppable in the face of opposition and struggle.

When I think of Namie and my mother, of Bintou's mother, her grandmother and all the women who raised me, I never see weakness. I see wisdom instead; foresight and fortitude. I see determination, courage, strength and fearlessness, no less from the women in my life than the men in my life. Perhaps, I see women differently because I grew up among them, sheltered and protected by them, nurtured and cared for, while the men of my family were mainly absent. My father left to go abroad to work when I was just two years old, leaving me in the warm embrace of the women of the family.

In that cocoon of compassion, where I was forced to stay, given my failing eyesight, I learned to be a man of compassion and consideration, to communicate, to compromise, to cajole. I learned that strong women were the norm. In fact, I don't think I have ever encountered a weak African woman. Ever!

Namie was a griot in her own right. She was more than a storyteller. She was a diplomat, a community leader, a counselor, a negotiator, a peacemaker, a problem solver, a beacon of light and love. Throughout my life, I witnessed her solve the unsolvable, settle erupting disputes and resolve long-simmering conflicts. She was a leader, not a follower; strong and never weak. I learned that feminine power is not always soft and supple; it can be forceful and even harsh, especially when the family is threatened.

As I grew into my manhood, I had a unique understanding of the power of women. In my research, I came across a landmark book by the iconoclast, Ashley Montagu, entitled *The Natural Superiority of Women*, in which he espouses the notion that the human species has evolved to its heights of development precisely because of women. Says Dr. Montagu, "Women are the mothers of humanity; do not let us ever forget that or underemphasize its importance. What mothers are to their children, so will man be to man."

He reminds us that, "Women are the carriers of the true spirit of humanity--the love of the mother for her child. Women are the bearers, the nurturers of life; men have more often tended to be the curtailers, the destroyers of life." My life confirms these notions of female power. More importantly, I learned that you don't have to be a weak man to love a strong woman; that we can complement one another and grow in equal strength and influence. Not one over the other, but both together. Furthermore, much of what I have learned from women has helped me navigate the tough terrain of immigration and taught me to be a better teacher, husband and friend.

As I gaze into Amina's darling eyes, I envision a woman as strong as her mother, her grandmothers and her great grandmother, whom she will never meet, but whom she will definitely come to know well. That is why Amina is named after her. As her father, I will raise her in the tradition of the women who raised me in Africa, even though she will know America as her home.

Every day, those women showed me that real strength, real courage comes not through sheer muscularity, rather, that strength lies at the crossroads of faith and fear. Namie always said, "We're all born with exactly what we need to fulfill our destiny." She was teaching me to be a real man.

Faith vs. Fear

Of all the lessons I learned from the women in my life, none was more essential to my development than the lesson of faith over fear. From early on, Namie drilled into my head that fear was my prime enemy. She would repeat, "Being scared is doing a disservice to the ultimate protector and provider of all the worlds!" over and over again. For she knew that if I were frightened of the world, I would never have a chance to survive in it, whether I could see or not, whether I could fight or not. Women like Namie knew it wasn't about strength, but about mental and moral fortitude. They armed me well!

They taught me that faith is the foundational requirement for all human advancement – personal and collective. My studies in history have confirmed the wisdom of my mothers. All great men and women accomplish great feats by first having the faith to see beyond the boundaries of low expectations. Great leaders take leaps of faith across chasms of common wisdom, often without seeing their landing point. Faith sparks the creative impulse and faith makes the fire burn brightly. Whatever your religious persuasion, most people can fully understand the meaning of faith described in Paul's letter to the Hebrews (known as the book of faith): "faith is the substance of things hoped for, the evidence of things not seen."

That is the power of faith; to project hope into reality without evidence in advance. What other force in nature has that ability? To be clear, I am not proposing some mystical notion of mind over matter. I am suggesting, instead, that we will never take risks (individually or as a people), move outside our comfort zones, and venture out into the world unless we have a positive view of the future and, if not a perfect future, then the ability to maneuver through uncertainty and complexity with success.

I was reminded of the importance of faith over fear when I showed up at my students' prom last year. This was beyond my comfort zone by any stretch of the imagination. In previous years, I would be worried about all sorts of things that could go wrong, such as falling down, missing my students' hand when they attempted a handshake or knocking someone's plate by accident, etc. But taking the leap of faith and showing up at that prom at night gave me the opportunity to experience how special life could be if we're able to move beyond the walls of the unseen.

In the fall of 2016, I took 23 of my students for a "Millionaire Mind Experience" weekend seminar in Philadelphia. The journey was a little difficult for me to maneuver at night. For example, standing at the 30th Street Station in Philadelphia, a couple of my students ran up to me saying, "Oh my God Mr., look at that beautiful building." As they were pointing to the left, I was looking in the opposite direction. And then, all of a sudden, they said, "What's wrong with you, Mr.?" Incidents like this occurred throughout the weekend and, yes, they were uncomfortable moments for me. However, my uncomfortable moments were nothing compared to the joy, transformation, and clear sense of direction that my students had that weekend.

The event started on Saturday morning at 9. Around 8am, all of the students came out of their hotel rooms dressed in their professional attire, each holding a folder with a pen and a composition notebook. After a quick stop at Starbucks, we headed to the conference room. As the students grabbed their nametags, they were ecstatic as the crowd stared at them, probably wondering "what are these kids doing here?"

It was an all-day event lasting until 7pm. After a nice dinner at Boston Market, we came back to the hotel. We gathered together as a group in a circle to debrief and reflect on the day. Each student was eager to share their experience. As we went around the circle, each of us shared our experience or memorable moment(s) from the day.

While everyone's experience was gratifying, I was struck by one of the students in the group who had low self-esteem issues. When it was her turn to speak, she paused and took a deep breath. "I learned a lot today, but it was also a very difficult day for me. I reflected on a lot of things I had not thought about. For example," she continued, "during the self-love activity, when the moderator said to write three things about what we like about ourselves, I could not come up with any."

After the group reflection was over, before heading to bed, I called the student so I could chat with her. As we sat on the floor in the hallway, I reminded her of some of the things that were special about her:

1. You are the most dedicated student I know

2. You are the most eloquent speaker in class

3. You are generous and kind-hearted

4. You have a gift of coming up with brilliant ideas in a split second

5. You possess a unique quality that most people don't: A sincerity of spirit which is the ultimate beauty

As I went through the different qualities she possessed, she said, "Mr., I know, but it is so unfair." What she meant by this was the passing of her father.

She grew up with an alcoholic father who was never present in her life. Without having the opportunity to know him, he passed away and this left a void in her life. She continued, "If I was beautiful or special, I would have meant somebody to him." This sense of abandonment had been the obstacle that this student could not overcome. We had a long conversation and I assured her that as the weekend progressed, she would learn ways to help her.

The Sunday morning started with a breakfast at, you guessed it, McDonalds. My wonderful colleague and I went to pick up the breakfast as the students were getting ready. They came out of their rooms looking sharp, grabbed their order and went down to the conference room. We were the first people to arrive because I didn't want them to miss the segment on Releasing the Past.

When the segment on releasing the past ended, the moderator shared a painful chapter in his life with us and a chill went down my spine. It was the same storyline as that of the student I spoke with the night before. His father was an alcoholic with whom he didn't have a meaningful relationship. He felt unloved by his father and as a result, developed an anger and hatred towards him. This anger stayed with him throughout his life.

An adult with children of his own, he didn't have a meaningful relationship with his children either. A few years ago, after conversations with different people, he realized that his current family problems were largely due to the anger and hatred he had in him about his father. While he would never forget about what happened to him, he decided to forgive his father. "And, boy, I haven't felt that light my whole life." He went on to explain the Nelson Mandela quote, "Resentment is like drinking poison and then hoping it will kill your enemies." At the end of sharing his story, he asked us to join him to sing a song that had helped him in his healing process. But before we sang the song together, he asked us to think of the people who have hurt us in the past that we're still holding onto.

Over three hundred people stood shoulder to shoulder holding hands, ready to release the past and moving towards a brighter future. The song was Mike and the Mechanics' "The Living Years." As we sang and wept, we were all reminded of our shortcomings in life and that we should never be a hostage of the actions of others. This was not because those individuals were bad, but because we haven't been in their shoes.

As the song concluded, we hugged each other knowing that there was a brighter future. The students came to me one at a time, their eyes filled with tears. They hugged me and whispered, "Thank you so much, Mr. Alhassan."

The moderator concluded that he would later learn from those who knew his father well that he grew up in an abusive environment. He never understood the meaning of love. He continued, "I was asking him to give me something he didn't have. How many of us actually do this in life?" he asked. "As I released my father of his shortcoming, I am able to be a better father to my kids today."

During the break, the student with whom I spoke the night before, came to me with her I pad, and said, "My mom wants to talk to you." Unfortunately, I did not speak Spanish, so all I understood was, "Mucha Gracias." I saw tears rolling down her eyes, but they were tears of joy. My student's mom was living in South America. When our conversation was over, she said, "My mom said to give you a hug for her."

Over the next few months, this student began to rebuild her life and her self-confidence. She graduated among the top students in her class. She is now in a relationship and attending a four year college. While all is not well, she accepted her place in this world.

Although I was worried about going on the trip to the seminar, what my student's gained from it far outweighed my fears. Always choose faith over fear. After all, both faith and fear rely on our imaginations. With fear, we imagine the worst outcome. With faith, we imagine the best. Since we don't know the future, it makes sense to move in the direction of light instead of darkness. One weapon of overcoming fear is to serve something bigger than you.

Peeling Cultural Cataracts and Understanding Cultural Evolution

Of all that I have discovered during my intercontinental journey, across a vast ocean, through a cultural time warp, from a small town with one dominate culture to a large nation with many diverse cultures and communities; I have learned that we often develop cultural cataracts, a condition in which the social lenses through which we see become increasingly opaque and blurry. This is not a condemnation, rather a simple recognition of reality.

Though I believe humans are naturally good, I realize we develop a worldview influenced by our surroundings. We inherit our prejudices and pride, not knowing that these views are neither the default, nor widely held. We simply live in a cultural bubble constructed by the world in which we are raised.

As an immigrant, I have had the unique opportunity to see both sides of this phenomenon. As I came to America, I was confronted with preconceived notions of what Americans were, of what Black Americans were, and White Americans, and women and men and children. Likewise, I was confronted with the preconceived notions Americans had of Africans, of immigrants, of Muslims, and black men, often negative and fearful.

When Andrew first met me, he saw a Black man. He assumed I would fit a mold he had formed in his mind about American blacks (lazy, late and leery of work). His experience was that the American black workers he hired to work in his grocery store rarely lasted a night or two. When he met me, he saw me through those cultural cataracts at first. But when he finally met me the man, he learned that I did not fit those preconceived notions and that I was a complex man with a story of my own. We grew to be great friends because he was willing to clean off those cultural smears and see me as an individual.

Likewise, I had learned to recognize my own cultural myopia and shortsightedness. I too have had to wipe my assumptions about black students in the inner city, white people everywhere and my own culture. This cultural reevaluation has made me a better teacher, a better husband and a better friend.

As a first year teacher, most of my troubles were centered on the lens through which I was looking. For example, most of my students were from the Dominican Republic. In the Dominican culture, hugs and kisses on the cheek are part of everyday life. I used to be so furious when students would be hugging each other in the morning before the bell rang because I thought it was inappropriate. So right at the beginning of the day, I set the wrong tone. Gee, no wonder why I could not effectively teach them because I was trying to rob them of their culture while imposing mine on them.

As I began to peel the cataract that blocks my ability to see that their culture could absolutely be compatible with my beliefs and understandings of the world, our relationship soared to a new height. I've come to learn that teaching is all about relationships. Therefore, it is imperative to adjust our cultural lenses to begin to create a more harmonious world.

As I have matured culturally, I have also recognized that culture is not cast in stone, rather it evolves and adapts over time. Whereas some believe in the orthodoxy, infallibility and immutability of culture, the reality is that cultures must shift in order to survive over time, given the simple limitations of time and space. This is not controversial, of course, as any cultural anthropologist will attest.

I point this out because I have seen it happen first hand. It became crystal clear to me when Amina was born, and my entire African clan was there assembled at the hospital. Here we were in a new country with new traditions and expectations. Literally, we were poised at the juncture of a new generation; a new child in a new world. Would the father remain with the expectant mother at the hospital or leave her mother with her, who had for thousands of generations, played this critical role? Ever so gently, without loud consternation, Bintou's mother acceded to me, giving way to a new order of things.

She was not replaced in her duties as the mother and grandmother. She was simply sharing those responsibilities with me. We are no less African for recognizing this small, though notable, change. And neither is Amina, who will become African in her American identity or more American in her African identity -- the blend, the swirl, the mixing of cultures, giving way to new cultures and traditions. This is how a people survive to tell their story.

The Power of Stories

As I began to talk about writing my story, many people would ask, "Why?"

I must confess there were moments when I would ask myself that same question, doubtful I had much to share in my short life. But my friends, who know my story because they know me, have often encouraged me to write down these stories. They tell me my stories inspire them and give them a sense of our common humanity, and at a simpler level, my friends tell me my stories are funny, instructive, informative, entertaining and, most importantly, interesting.

In helping me work through the purpose of this narrative venture, my friends brought me back to my roots, guided me home, like a lost boy. There I found the true purpose and power of the story itself, there embedded in my very DNA: the story for the sake of the story itself. Stories and storytelling and story tellers are the sinew and structure of civilization itself, without which we would only have dried bones and silent stones to know from which we came.

Civilization would not have advanced, cultures formed, without stories. Literature would not be born and humanity would not have an identity and a soul without Homer, Confucius, Shakespeare, Achebe,

Garcia Lorca, Bamba Susso, etc. Our stories are our most important treasures as a people and our most valuable gifts to one another.

The story is the blues, the ballad, the battle hymn, sermon, scripture, the aria, the prayer. From the time a primitive people sat around the fireplace at night, our faces aglow, the darkness behind us, we would tell one another something called a story.

In much of West Africa, we have a tradition of introducing a story. The storyteller hollers, "Story! Story!" And the listeners reply in eager anticipation, accepting the generous offer, "Story!" In my language of Mandinka, it translates, "Ntaling! Ntaling!" and we respond, "Ntaling Dima!" Please tell us the story. It is what Amina says every night before her shoulders slump to sleep, "Daddy, mommy, story time!" as she hands us a stack of books.

It is what we do when we are together, whether old or young, rich or poor, able to speak or not. We turn to one another and look into each other's faces and tell our stories. That is why I tell my story.

The need to share stories is as human and fundamental as breathing itself. We first learn to tell our own stories before we learn to re-tell the stories of others. It is how we relate to one another on a personal basis. It is these individual stories which are woven together into a wide tapestry of human civilization and history. Our stories are as important as each of us. They fit together into a patchwork of humanity. My story, Your story, Our story.

That is why your story is as important as the story of a wealthy king, the most beautiful movie star, or bravest soldier returning home from war. As I share my story, therefore, I encourage you to share yours, as well. We have the obligation to share our sorrows, our success, our sadness, the triumphs, tribulations, tributes, the stories and the lessons we can impart to the next generation so we can move inexorably into a more enlightened future together.

In that sense, we are all griots and we are all the griots' son.

The Meaning of Pain

Dr. Wayne Dyers' mantra about life is an excellent segue into looking at the meaning of pain, "If you change the way you look at things, the things you look at change."

I once heard someone define pain in this eloquent and thoughtful manner:

P: Pay

A: Attention

I: Inside

N: Now

Pain is inevitable. It is part of humanity, and it can serve a higher purpose if managed well. As I told my student at the beginning of this book, we can either go through pain or grow through it. Pain will change us, but how it changes us is up to us.

It could be our complicated bosses whom we can never seem to satisfy, negative coworkers, an abusive spouse, or a physical illness, like mine, that we feel is preventing us from thriving and reaching our destiny.

Or maybe it is a combination of some or all of these things. All of these are difficult to bear, but none of them happened by accident. They happened to us to help us develop our character and get to our next level. Just as the definition of PAIN indicates, if we would pay attention to what's happening inside, and allow our character to develop, then we'd come out of the situation better. Painful experiences of life are only a tragedy if we allow them to be. We can turn any pain in our lives into an opportunity. Examples that I usually highlight to my students about turning pain into opportunity are: If you fail an exam, that does not mean you're a failure, instead, it gives a feedback on what skills you need to develop. If you caught people talking negatively about you, and it bothers you, that is a sign that you need to work on your self-esteem and self-confidence. Once you acquire these skills, then you will not worry about others talking about you. As Eleanor Roosevelt said, "Small minds, discuss people; Average minds, discuss events; Great minds, discuss ideas." Therefore, next time you hear someone speaking badly about you, just recognize that that person has a small mind.

Unfortunately, most of the time, we do not understand the presence of adversity or a challenge in our life. When I first discovered my vision challenges, I thought my life would have no meaning. In fact, I thought I would live my life in defeat and would not amount to much. Sadly, for most of my life, this was my reality. It was my reality because I allowed it to control my life. Every setback in our life can result in a setup for a greater comeback. But the key is that we must create the condition to allow it.

Is my vision cured? No. Is it better than it ever was? Not at all. Do I have the same struggles that I did before? Absolutely. For example, as a teacher, there is always tons of paperwork: from grading, to creating lesson plans, PowerPoint, activity guides, etc. Each of these requires a tremendous amount of time on the computer. And looking at the computer screen for a bit does cause watery eyes, irritation, and itching for me. Preparing for lessons and setting up my classroom for the day's lessons takes me longer than most of my colleagues. I typically get to school at 7:45am, an hour and 15 minutes before school starts to give myself enough time to get ready. My day usually ends at 6pm. The two hours after classes are over are my preparation time, meeting with students, and running after school programs. But, at the end of the day, I get home fulfilled knowing that I made a contribution.

I was reminded of this at the end of the 2015-16 school year when I was teasing a student who will be in my class as a senior next year. Her name is Mariama. I asked, "What did you hear about my class?" The answer I was expecting was, "too much homework," since that's what most of my students warn the upcoming class about. Instead she replied "Do you want me to be honest?" I said, "That'd be helpful." She replied:

> "Well, at the beginning of the school year last year, a group of us were hanging out, and I told my friends that I had no idea what I wanted to do with my life. As soon as I said that, all the students who had taken your class told me not to worry as I would figure it out once I got to your class."

She then continued, "That's what I am looking forward to in your class next year." I was stunned and silent. I replied, "Well, that's not the answer I was expecting, but I'm looking forward to having you in class next year."

This is the central reason for the production of this book. That we're not defined by our condition but rather the choices we make despite our condition rather than because of it. Viktor Frankl said it best in his remarkable book, *Man's Search for Meaning*, "To live is to suffer, to survive is to find meaning in your suffering."

Comfort vs. Conviction

It is easier to do what is comfortable because it generally does not need stretching of the boundaries of your life. However, true and lasting happiness lies not in what is familiar, but within the walls of the unknown. Comfortable is meeting expectations of reality. But in order for us to live a compelling life, we need to be consistently making progress. Whatever area of our lives we're unhappy with, we're typically not progressing in that area. If comfort means doing what is familiar, then what is conviction?

Conviction means pushing into the unknown. By following our convictions in making the decisions of our lives, this will shape our destiny. In the past few years, I've been getting out of my comfort zones, and by doing so, I am able to have experiences beyond my imagination.

A recent example of this for me took place a few months ago. I flew to Phoenix for a seminar not knowing what to expect in regard to the room setting. As always, visiting new places always brings a challenge for me, especially if I am not traveling with my wife.

On a typical day, I would go in early when the lights are brighter inside before the program begins. However, my flight was delayed, so when I entered the arena, it was pitch black. Everything was dark except the stage. I paused, thinking, how in the world am I going to find a seat? As I stood there contemplating on what to do, security asked me to leave that area. Looking confused and not knowing what to do, I slowly started to make my way down the stairs. I luckily found a seat at the second row from the top. That was good enough for me even though I bought a VIP ticket and should have been in the front on the floor of the arena.

Was that a difficult seminar to maneuver? You bet. Throughout the day, I had missteps and uncomfortable moments. However, the knowledge I gained and the people I met led me to develop a program for my students that takes place twice a week before school. I could not have imagined how that program would transform my students' view of themselves and others as well as create a compelling future for themselves and their families.

The program I developed was called the "Teens Future." It was a voluntary program that took place on Tuesdays and Thursdays before school. It looked at five areas of life: Attitude, Goals and Vision, Communication and Interpersonal Skills, and Leadership and Financial Literacy. When I first proposed the idea to my principal, she was on board as long as I could maintain at least 5 students who would consistently attend. Some of my colleagues had already attempted before-school programs, but had to cancel due to low attendance. In addition, the program was launching in the middle of winter, so the expectation of teenagers waking up extra early in freezing weather was unrealistic.

I am a firm believer that we should never set our expectations to meet the reality of others but that we should always go with our conviction to meet our destiny. So with this in mind, I went ahead and presented the idea to the students. A significant number of them signed up but I could only take a maximum of 33 students. When I brought the applications to my principal, she was pleasantly surprised but cautioned me that while the number of applicants was impressive, it might not necessarily mean that they would all show up. Regardless, she supported the program because she has a sense of service and passion that allows the teachers to go above and beyond what is required of them to serve the students' best interest.

I launched "Teens Future" in the first week of January. To my surprise, the whole group of students showed up on the first week. Week after week, month after month, regardless of rain, snow, ice or zero degree temperatures, they showed up consistently for the rest of the school year. In fact, only three students had inconsistent attendance of which two had family related issues.

The results at the end of the program were gratifying: All the graduating seniors in the program will be attending college in the fall of 2016. More importantly, they all knew what they wanted to do with their lives through their personal, professional and social contribution goals. Each one of them had a vision board and a goal statement with a financial action plan for attaining their goals. While all these are phenomenal achievements, nothing is more important to me than the transformation in how they feel about themselves and how that translates into having a better relationship with their families and others.

The students became more than just classmates and friends. They became each other's coach and accountability partners. Some embarked on a weight loss journey together, others partnered up for better family relationships, etc. Three times a week, they would call or text to check on their partners' progress. My role became more of a facilitator than a teacher. They took charge of their own personal development and transformation. They found the class to be so valuable that during spring break, we did a two full day seminar on communication and leadership. Not only did the students show up, they stayed the entire time on both days.

This was a far cry from just three years earlier, when I could not get more than two students to stay for after school tutoring. How did I go from students running away from me to now "hiding" in order to get a few minutes of quiet time? I realized that I was hoping for fewer problems instead of striving for more problem-solving skills; I was hoping that the situation was magically going to get easier, rather than me striving to become a better person and teacher. For the situation between my students and me to change, I had to change.

One thing remains to be true, students will not learn from people they don't like. No meaningful learning can take place in an environment where the connection between the teacher and the students, is not built on mutual understanding and mutual respect. One of my students, Julio, reminded me while I was explaining that in order to have a meaningful relationship with others, we need to strive to make the other person feel important, "Mr. do you know why I used to give you a hard time your first year?" I said "No." He continued, "You never paid attention to me, but whenever I disrupted your class, you had no choice but to give me the attention I wanted." To feel important or significant is not a desire or want, but a universal need of all people. When Julio told me this, it was during his senior year. We had developed a close relationship since that terrible first year. I taught Julio for three consecutive years, and I could not be more proud of being his teacher due to the transformation he went through. I had to develop the skills necessary to help my students to excel.

Now, I know that human connection is far more superior to any curriculum we deem important.

These remarkable changes in my students would probably not have happened if I stayed in my comfort zone. As I struggle with my continuous biological vision loss, I am fulfilled with the vision of transforming the lives of people who are put in my path. While none of my students knew of my vision challenges, they continued to view me as a symbol of hope and inspiration.

My sincere hope is that you were able to find meaning in these short episodes of my life to strive for the best in your life. As I get older, I realize one thing: when I am worried, sad, depressed, frustrated, guilty, fearful etc. about my vision challenges, it typically is all about me. But my joyous and fulfilling moments happen in service to others. Despite every challenge I have faced and continue to face due to my sight or lack of it, I have every tool I need to succeed and to live a meaning life. The more I learn and understand the world, the better I can see…

The End

ACKNOWLEDGMENT

My sincere gratitude goes to every one of you for taking this journey with me. It is difficult to thank everyone who has made a difference in my life by name, but I want you to know that each encounter has been a blessing in my life and has shaped who I am today.

I'd never be where I am today if it wasn't for the nurturing and caring of my parents, Alhaji Papa Susso and Sarjo Jobarteh. Thank you Dad and Mom for everything.

To my siblings: Sankung, Fatou and A.K. Susso, you taught me the meaning of family and friendship. It's always great to be in the company of thoughtful and loving individuals who I can always count on during times of celebration or sorrow.

To my phenomenal sister-in-law, Amy Marie Susso, to whom I owe a debt of gratitude for being my guiding force whenever I go off track, thank you for all you do to find solutions to most of the family challenges.

For watching Amina while I write this book, thank you Jatou for your patience and nurturing abilities that contributed to giving me the freedom to get this project done. On the same token, I want to thank my amazing sister-in-law, Mariama, for teaching me the meaning of compassion, love and family.

To my brilliant brother-in-law: Dawda, thank you for helping to enhance my technological skills, which became crucial during the creation of this book, and for inspiring me to write my story.

To my fabulous mother-in-law: your cheerfulness, tenacity and responsibility keep our household smooth. Thank you for your consistent support since the day I became a part of your family. And to my father-in-law: thank you for your support. You are an inspiration to all of us.

To Dr. Steward Pickett: thank you for your friendship, academic support, encouragement, and guidance. My life has turned out much better for knowing you.

I am forever indebted to all the great educators who paved the way for me. Special thanks to Ms. Felter, Ms. Wiley and Professor Holmes.

I would not be where I am today personally and professionally without the unyielding support of my Market America family. Without you, this book would probably not have happened. You were the people who gave me the belief that with discipline, the attainment of any dream is possible. With your encouragement, I found my voice and a clear sense of direction.

To my International Community High School family: thank you for the joyous, as well as, the painful experiences. It was at ICHS that my character began to develop.

A special thank you to my Principal: Berena Carbacas, for your continued support and mentorship.

To my "brother" and friend, Ousseynou Ndiaye: thank you for your constant guidance and support. It is always crucial to have a trusted friend in the workplace and you have superseded that expectation.

To my first unofficial mentor, Didi: thank you for your compassion and caring attitude during my times of difficulty. It was great to know that I have someone who will always listen to me.

Thank you to my wonderful "sisters:" Ms. Lopez, Ms. Nadia, Ms. Irma, Ms. Yvonne, Ms. Joseph for always making me laugh and being there when I needed you.

To my Social Studies Department: thank you for constantly engaging in the sharing of meaningful ideas. On the same token, to my Team MNOP family: thank you for giving me the opportunity to lead. It was through this experience that my leadership abilities were enhanced.

Thank you to Kevin Morris for your patience, thoughtfulness and attention to detail while editing the book.

Thank you Sue Manocha and Kristen Meltzer for proof reading and to Mory Rivera for making the book stand out through its pictorial representation. To Irma, Jonathan and Craig: thank you for the countless hours spent on helping with the design.

My deepest gratitude goes to my best friend and partner, Bintou. Ever since I met you, my life has been transformed for the better. Having you in my life taught me patience, compassion, tolerance and understanding. Thank you for sharing this journey of life with me.

ABOUT THE AUTHOR

Alhassan Susso is an educator, speaker and author who has devoted his career to transforming the lives of young people facing difficulties, particularly new immigrants to America. An immigrant from West Africa, Alhassan came to America as a teenager coping with a rare eye disease which left him nearly blind at an early age.

Having overcome this and other obstacles, Mr. Susso seeks to expand the worldview of young minds so they could find meaning in their lives in order for them to reach their destiny.

As a high school teacher at a New York City Public School specializing in educating new immigrants, Alhassan has worked with children from all across the globe, facing a range of personal, social and economic challenges. Drawing on his own personal struggles, Alhassan has honed his talent for engaging students at their level and helping them transform their lives.

Over the past several years, he has worked with over 600 teens. His electrifying smile, energy and authenticity have earned him the moniker of "The most admired and influential teacher."

37506738R00132

Made in the USA
San Bernardino, CA
31 May 2019